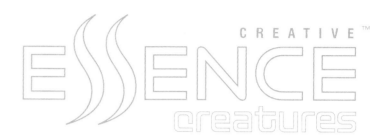

CREATIVE™
ESSENCE
creatures

D1605245

JAMES VAN DEN BOGART

Ballistic Publishing
Finest digital art in the known universe

FRONT COVER IMAGE CREDITS

**ANDREW BAKER
& SIMON WEBBER**
Initial concepts and sculpt

JOSH HERMAN
Final sculpt

IAN JOYNER
Polypaint and render

BACK COVER IMAGE CREDITS

**ARIS KOLOKONTES
& MARTIN REZARD**
Initial concepts and sculpt

JAMES VAN DEN BOGART
Final sculpt

BRYAN WYNIA
Polypaint and render

134 Gilbert St | Adelaide SA 5000 | Australia
correspondence: info@ballisticpublishing.com
www.BallisticPublishing.com

First Edition published in Australia 2013 by Ballistic Publishing
Softcover/Slipcase Edition   ISBN 978-1-921828-99-7

PUBLISHER: Ballistic Publishing
EDITORS: Mark Thomas and Kathy Sharrad
SENIOR DESIGNER: Mark Thomas

PRINTING AND BINDING: Everbest Printing (China): www.everbest.com

PARTNERS: The CGSociety (Computer Graphics Society): www.CGSociety.org

SOCIETY OF DIGITAL ARTISTS

Visit www.BallisticPublishing.com for our complete range of titles.

FSC
www.fsc.org
100%
Paper from well-managed forests
FSC® C021256

JOSH HERMAN

CREATIVE™
ESSENCE
creatures

BRYAN WYNIA : ANDREW BAKER : ARIS KOLOKONTES

IAN JOYNER : JAMES VAN DEN BOGART : JOSH HERMAN

MARTIN REZARD : SIMON WEBBER

/ BALLISTIC /

introduction ∎

The *Creative Essence* series sets a benchmark for professional and aspiring artists, giving inspiration to all who aim for greatness in the CG industries. The series is for anyone who wants to delve more deeply into understanding the techniques and processes behind creating stunning digital art – whether for games, films or private work. The series takes you well beyond most tutorial books by providing you with an insight into the creative techniques and decision-making processes employed by our selected master artists.

The first book in the *Creative Essence* series is the best-selling *Creative Essence: The Face*, which shows how six professionals created a digital model of a face from beginning to end. *The Face* encompasses reference photography, modeling, UV mapping, texturing and rendering to create a digital double that would be at home in any next-generation game, cinematic or movie.

Creative Essence: Creatures is the definitive book on sculpting creatures and takes the series to another level. It features the private work of some of the best creature concept artists and 3D modelers working in the CG industries today. The *Creative Essence* series provides the perfect platform for our artists to excel at what they do best. In this volume we present the amazing results that were achieved when our artists had the chance to discard the constraints of a commercial studio's production process. They took up our offer of having complete creative freedom and just ran with it – genius or madness – you can judge for yourselves (we think it's genius).

Featuring page upon page of never-before-seen artwork – from doodles and pencil sketches to dynamic concept paintings, exploratory maquettes, 3D sculpting and modeling and final rendering – this book reveals the essence of each artist's creative process. This is an unprecedented exploration of these artists' decision-making processes, and a stunning visual record – a vivid cornucopia of previously un-imagined creatures.

FROM BALLISTIC PUBLISHING AND THE CG SOCIETY

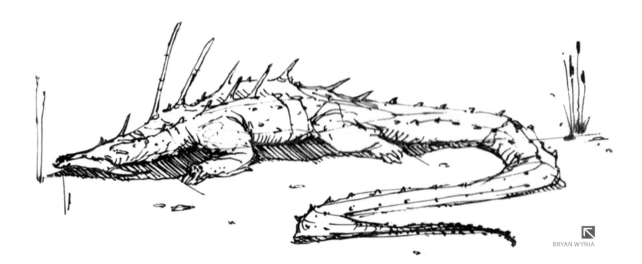

BRYAN WYNIA

The 256 pages of this book feature work specially commissioned from our group of eight artists – Bryan Wynia, Andrew Baker, Aris Kolokontes, Ian Joyner, James Van Den Bogart, Josh Herman, Martin Rezard and Simon Webber. Their list of production credits includes killer game and film titles such as *God of War: Ascension, The Amazing Spider-Man, World War Z, Snow White and the Huntsman, Thor: The Dark World, Harry Potter and the Deathly Hallows, Prometheus, Gladiator, The Matrix* and *The Hobbit* trilogy. Each of these artists was hand-picked on the strength of their reputation, diverse creative style, and widely varied approach to creative and production processes.

Creative Essence: Creatures exposes the thoughts and decisions behind each artist's work – what happens when they stare at a blank page; where they look for inspiration; how they incorporate reference material into their concepts; how they analyze their concepts and decide what needs refining and what needs deleting; what their process of development is; and the variety of techniques they employ to bring their concept to stunning visual resolution.

One of the most important skills a digital artist needs is the ability to create something believable. Each artist has created a number of incredible creatures, and you can follow each of them through from initial concept – whether in pencil, clay or directly in a 3D package – to final render. Our artists have created an array of very believable creatures, some you might want to cuddle and some you certainly wouldn't want to meet on a dark night…

Bryan Wynia has been the North American backbone of this whole project, and he deserves recognition here for his efforts. His enthusiasm for the initial concept helped launch the book, and throughout the entire process he was a vital touch-point for the other artists as well as producing an amazing body of work himself. His involvement has made the entire process much smoother than it may otherwise have been – so massive thanks go to him.

Our aim at Ballistic Publishing is not simply to publish books, but to craft gems – treasured objects of desire – and thousands of readers across many years have sought them out to own and display them. *Creative Essence: Creatures* is no exception, and presents a bewildering line up of creatures that we know you'll love. We are proud to present it to you.

/ BALLISTIC /

SOCIETY OF DIGITAL ARTISTS

the artists .

What follows is an amazing array of creatures from an amazing line up of artists. To dream these creatures up is one thing, being able to bring them to life is quite another. Our eight leading creature concept artists show off their very impressive talents with flying jellyfish, pipe-smoking aliens, fungus eaters, evil science experiments, egg thieves and one very, very large squid ...

70
aris kolokontes
The Hobbit trilogy, *Dr Who, Elysium*

108
ian joyner
The Amazing Spider-Man, Snow White and the Huntsman, Cowboys and Aliens

170
josh herman
Avengers, Iron Man 3, Uncharted 3: Drake's Deception

200
martin rezard
Harry Potter and the Deathly Hallows, Prometheus, Game of Thrones

230
simon webber
Pacific Rim, The Amazing Spider-Man, Avatar

the cover.

TEAM ONE
INITIAL CONCEPT AND SCULPT
ARIS KOLOKONTES

I started this the same way I begin thinking about creating any creature, and ask myself if it will be a bust or a full body sculpt. I tried to come up with some interesting looking shapes as well as a variety of forms that incorporate real-life animal elements. I chose this concept as it has a shark-like feel to it. As well as establishing the initial form, I tried to keep it rough enough for James to build on and take to a finished sculpt.

TEAM ONE
FINAL SCULPT
JAMES VAN DEN BOGART

Aris's beautiful work gave me a ton of secondary forms to build on. I made small tweaks to the overall shape of the head and made the jaw much shorter. Most of the work I did was in the details and refining interior shapes. I wanted to give Bryan some fun materials and textures to play with. I added hard plating on the top of the head and also some bumps and wrinkles on the creature's underside to illustrate softer skin. I also sculpted an exposed clavicular protrusion. I was thinking the protrusion might creep in from the bottom of the image and lead the viewer's eye to the face.

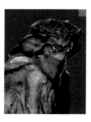

TEAM ONE
POLYPAINT AND FINAL RENDER
BRYAN WYNIA

The guys gave me a great design sculpt to start from. It was really inspiring to collaborate on this creature with them. I started by exploring various color options, and in the end we decided to move forward with a greenish-red palette. At this point I embraced the direction in which the creature was heading, and gathered my own reference material including images of a variety of amphibians and scientific paintings of dinosaurs. It was very important that color theory tied in with the forms and the overall design of the creature.

Two teams in a competitive collaboration created two busts for the cover. Each artist only had a few days to do their part before passing their work up the line. Aris, Martin, James and Bryan formed Team One and Andrew, Simon, Josh and Ian made up Team Two. Aris and Martin, from Team One, each presented their team with an initial sculpt, while Andrew and Simon (Team Two) did the same for their team. Both teams then chose one sculpt to go on to the next stages in the process. Which cover would you have chosen?

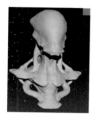

TEAM TWO INITIAL CONCEPT AND SCULPT
ANDREW BAKER

The cover image idea started off from a sphere and not much else. I knew I wanted to try something with negative space – an idea that evolved into imagining a faceless, translucent creature with some kind of bioluminescence. I was keen to see what the other artists up the line would do with the bust I created … needless to say, it turned out awesome!

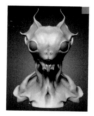

TEAM TWO FINAL SCULPT
JOSH HERMAN

I took this wacky but very cool-looking sketch of Andrew's and fleshed it out to a refined sculpt. The tubes that Andrew made provided some really interesting negative shapes around the creature's neck and shoulders, and immediately drew me to it. Initially, I was going to do something very bug-like, like a mantis or dragonfly, but I ended up keeping the large eyes and went with something more demonic and/or sci-fi. My goal was to keep some of Andrew's original shapes and to pull an interesting character out of it. I also wanted to establish a relationship between our creature and the viewer.

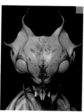

TEAM TWO POLYPAINT AND FINAL RENDER
IAN JOYNER

After Josh finished sculpting Andrew's awesome sketch, I realized that I wanted to focus on the frontal view of this creature. I love the giant eyes Josh created as well as the negative space created by the tubes that Andrew added, so I focused on those features. Since this was going to be for the cover, I wanted to go with a really striking color design. I went with the classic red and white and then pulled in some green/blue for the eyes. It was a lot of fun to work with these two talented guys and bring this fun little creature to life!

the process .

This is a book about creatures, and documents the entire process of imagining, drawing, modeling and sculpting them, and, ultimately, breathing life into them. While the artists tread similar creative paths, their journeys are never the same. We know it can be terrifying to stare at a blank page and not know where that lightning bolt of inspiration will come from. Here, we present a record of the unique processes that our master artists employ – to help inspire you on your own creative journey.

Imagine having a map to some of the most incredible creative minds at work in the CG industries today, available to hold, study and enjoy. In the following pages you can see how each artist responded to a simple brief, and the amazing tangents they went off on. Each artist's response to that brief led to a dizzying number of unique, but related, creations.

We developed a simple 'Creature Matrix' and then challenged our band of artists with it. It wasn't really a design brief, but more a starting point for their thinking. It was as simple as asking 'hunter or hunted?' and 'predator or prey?' Then we stood back to see what spectacular creatures would come to life as a result.

BRYAN WYNIA

What kind of predator might they be? What kind of prey are they? Do they lope, slither, leap, fly or plod? Are they furry, hairy, scaly or plated with armor? Do they evade their attackers with stealth, speed or strength? Do they use found weapons or something from their own natural armory to defend themselves? Where might they live – in a desert, jungle, ocean or in space?

IAN JOYNER

Are they prehistoric, contemporary or future dwellers? Are they mythical or reminiscent of real animals – or a combination of both? The results are as fascinating as they are varied.

Each artist then developed a back story to their creatures. Pondering a question about how a particular creature foraged for food would lead the artist to consider what kind of jaw line and musculature that creature might develop as a result. What kind of prey they hunt would give answers to questions about physical body types – are they built for speed (lean and sleek) or built for power (massive and solid)? Large heads rely on powerful shoulders to carry them; a predator requires intelligence to capture a poisonous but tasty prey.

It was a tantalizing invitation for the artists to focus their gaze beyond the horizon and bring into being all manner of new life forms. These creatures have never existed but it's easy to imagine that they could have, or do.

During the production of this book, we established a private blog where the artists could post work-in-progress images and get feedback from the other artists on the creatures they were developing. It became a rich melting pot of ideas, and some creatures were developed in direct response to other artist's creatures. See Bryan's Bog Bomber devouring Josh's Red-finned Slark on pages 36–37.

We also interviewed each artist about their creatures, and their insights and perspectives are presented in detailed interviews. The work-in-progress images are accompanied by captions written by the artists themselves, and provide further insight into their thought processes and decision-making.

As a final treat, each artist's group of finished creatures is complemented with an array of other concepts, from pencil sketches, early sculpts to almost-finished creatures that may appear somewhere, some time in the future.

On with the show…

MARTIN REZARD

bryan wynia

I grew up on a steady diet of monster movies, video games and comic books. There was something really interesting to me about making things people have never seen before. I remember at a young age finding some books on special make-up effects at a local magic shop. I would sit in there forever and read about Rick Baker, Stan Winston, Tom Savini and Steve Johnson. It suddenly hit me that these guys made monsters for a living. From that point on, I put all of my focus into making monsters.

My parents were really supportive and bought me some of the books and masks from the magic shop. I would go home and experiment and try some of the things I had read about. In high school I would put on these massive haunted house productions in my parents' backyard, until we started growing out of the space and a friend suggested I get a job at a local haunted house. A few days later I was working at Netherworld Haunted House. I consider this to be my 'big break' and still work with them after so many years. Netherworld exposed me to some of the most talented artists in the south-east, many of whom worked in film and television and were always very kind with sharing their knowledge.

I was a pretty awful student and after high school I was not sure what to do next. My parents suggested art school, and I thought it would be a good back-up plan to my path to become a make-up effects artist. To my surprise, attending art school was another big step for me. The Art Institute of Atlanta exposed me to all of these great

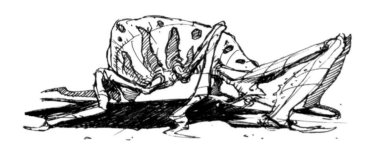

tools, techniques and theories. It was during this time that I first started experimenting with digital art and working in 3D.

I also worked at Lone Wolf FX as a make-up effects artist. I think this combination of school and studio experience really helped push and motivate me. During my senior year at the Art Institute, I landed an internship at Gentle Giant Studios in Burbank, California. This then lead to me and my now wife moving to Los Angeles as I continued to pursue my dream of making monsters.

Bill 'Splat' Johnson, the owner of Lone Wolf FX, is my mentor and I still call him today for advice. I learned more working in his shop than I would ever have learned in any school or reading any book. An instructor I had at the Art Institute named Elio Guevara is another mentor. Elio pushed me so much that at the time I may have hated him for it, but he helped me think outside of the box and explore new ideas. These two artists are such an important part of my life and I owe so much to both of them. I think their influences plus a heavy dose of midnight monster movies have helped create my style.

I recently left Sony Santa Monica where I was a Senior Character Artist. While at Sony, I created characters and creatures for *God of War: Ascension*. I now work at High-Rez Studios as a Senior Artist. The majority of my day is spent sculpting characters and

creatures either for concept or game assets. There is also a large amount of tea to be drunk during my typical work day.

When I'm not creating art for clients, I like to explore my own ideas and stories. As any good nerd does, I also love playing games, watching movies and collecting model kits. I also make pizza, which is honestly just a sad attempt to become a teenage mutant ninja turtle.

My advice to young artists: Focus on what you like. I meet students who try and be generalists, and I feel this can sometimes be limiting. Find out what you really want to do and strive to be the best at it. The industry today is an incredibly saturated and competitive market. You can find so many talented people online and you can work from all corners of the world. The hard part is getting your work out there and into the right hands.

In the future I hope to spend more time and energy on creating my own creatures and stories. I will also continue to eat pizza until I'm officially accepted into the ranks of the ninja turtles. I think you could sum up this entire biography into this: I was born in the 1980s and I like monsters.

rhinodino

Q: Talk a bit about some of the sketches you did in the early stages of working on this creature.

The first set of sketches, and even the majority of the second set of sketches, are of very large, hulking creatures. When I started with the Creature Matrix and came up with that idea, I had a very clear vision of what the final creature was going to be, but I didn't want to be locked into that. I wanted to be able to shoot off in completely different directions and explore all sorts of ideas. If I hadn't had the freedom to explore those different paths, it could have been detrimental to the character in the end.

The nice thing about doing thumbnails is that even if they don't contribute to the final creature, and you are taken down a path that leads to a dead end for that creature, it could be a starting point for another creature. So, whether it's for another creature in this book or if I got a freelance call one day saying, "Hey, we've got this idea for this weird quadruped, sick, feral dog-type thing…", I could go back and look at these sketches and use them as a springboard for another design.

Q: When you first started this creature, what was your end goal?

When we first started this book, the majority of us were using the Creature Matrix to come up with a set of designs. I know with my first creature I wanted to do a massive herbivore/omnivore type thing, something that lived in a herd, but the main thing I had in my mind was that I wanted to do something that was pretty believable, something that felt prehistoric but not totally from our world. This creature would have lived on a distant galaxy very similar to Earth during that planet's prehistoric time. Or, if we did find fossils of this creature on Earth, it could almost fit into our prehistoric time – that epoch when dinosaurs were fading out and the mammals were coming into play. The power plays that were going on then, I've always found really interesting. I wanted this creature to fit in that gap.

Q: What was your main inspiration for this creature?

A rhinoceros, because I love their social interaction, I love their size … there are a lot of things to rhinos that I find really interesting – the form and shapes of the body, the horns. Every little kid is pumped by rhinos and dinosaurs. When I first started thinking about this creature, I took my daughter to the LA Zoo and there was a rhino there. At that stage I knew what I wanted to make but I had no idea what it'd look like. I always take my camera with me to snap photos … and I took it with me to take photos at the zoo that day. This rhino did a turnaround for me, it just stood there so I could take photos of it at different angles.

Q: Looking at the sketches, there are rhino shapes but there are other inspirations coming through also. What else were you exploring?

When I'm working on creatures like this, that are kind of realistic, I try to find some animals that are real to ground it, so the viewer has some sense of familiarity when they look at it. But the difficult part is how you go about bringing something new to your creature, so it's not just a rhino that's blue, for example. So I started looking at hippos, pigs, and even at a few reptiles for inspiration. I knew I wanted to have a really clear distinction between the tool on the front of its head – a clear distinction between materials, like a moose with the antlers going into the furry body. Even though this character doesn't have fur, I wanted to have that really clear distinction between the tool and its body. That then started to take me out of the realm of it being just a fantasy rhino.

I try to do percentages with my creatures. The creature might be 40 percent rhino, 40 percent hippo and 20 percent chicken, for example. That last 20 percent could be something so random that it might be just the skin quality of a chicken or its coloring or a suggestion of movement.

Q: When you envisioned the Rhinodino, how did you see the axe part of his head and the tongue?

When designing a creature, one of the first questions I ask myself is how does it eat. The way I envisioned this creature

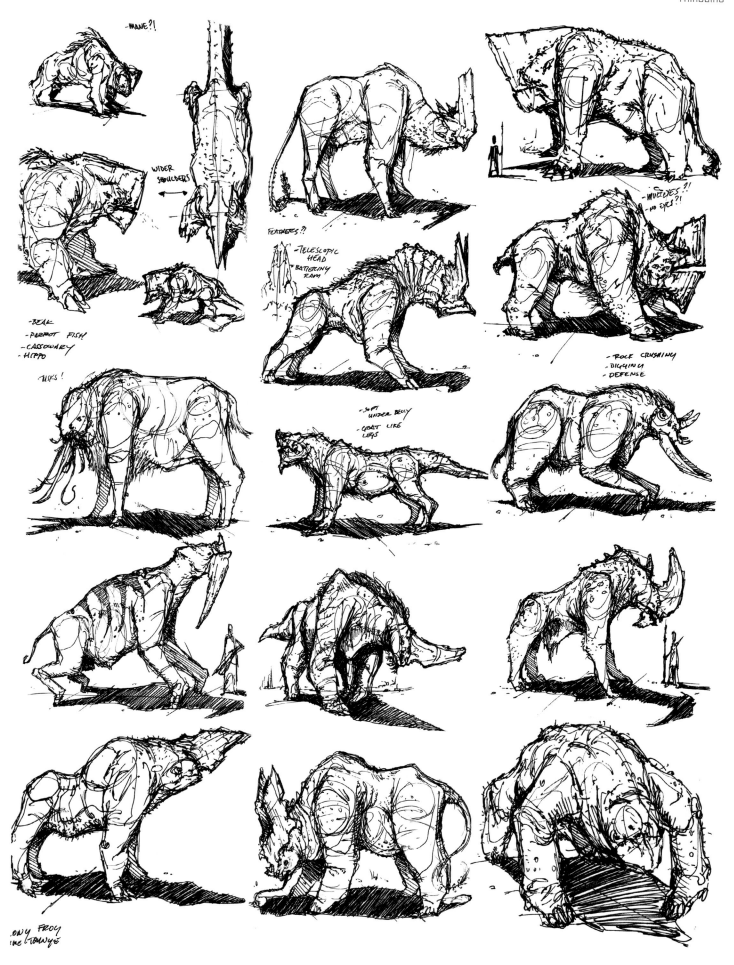

eats is that it uses its head's bony antler protrusion as a tool. In some of the sketches, this tool looks like an axe, a knife, a can opener. For some of those images, I looked at actual tools, like gardening tools – a rake or a spade. This creature has a really large, heavy head, which tells us that it eats closer to the ground, unlike creatures with a longer necks, like giraffes.

Also, I thought about the place this creature inhabits … there are these hard, rocky mounds, almost like termite mounds, and it uses its head to smash open these insect mounds to expose the food inside – fungus, bug larvae or whatever. It then uses its tongue to reach down in there and get the food. This is where the 20 percent inspiration comes in … I saw a diagram of a hummingbird skull and its tongue, which originates from between its eyes and wraps around inside the skull and comes out its mouth almost like a tape measure.

Q: After you've got a fairly good idea of a direction for your creature, what's the next thing you do – after your pencil sketches?

For this one, I took two of the pencil sketches that were speaking to me the most and I roughed them out in ZBrush (see image on page 12). These were really fast sculpts, done just to translate the 2D sketch into 3D to see what reads. At that point, the one on the left (with the more tool-shaped head, the large, lumbering creature), spoke to me the most, so I took that to the next step.

Q: In the head studies, we can see you tried out different shapes for the lips and shapes of the tools and eye positions…

Yes. A friend of mine taught me a saying that has always stuck in my head, especially to do with design work – that you should never leave a drawing in the ink well. That means that there are so many times that a designer will do a sketch and the first one they do they'll think that one will be it. But after you do 50 sketches, the first one is often so far from what you end up with. Even if they are not what you go with, they still contribute to the final design. I think it's important to explore as much as possible.

Q: Then you started playing around with textures like armor-plating, heavy skin and warts, bumps, spikes, etc. Did you have a direction you wanted to go in, or were you still just playing around?

I was still exploring at that point. I was thinking about his environment – was it a desert, so does he need really thick skin to store water, or does he live in grasslands with really aggressive, spiny thorns? Another question I asked myself besides what does this creature eat is what eats this creature. So he has these rigid horns down his back that act as a defensive mechanism to deter larger creatures from attacking him.

Q: So, there are other predatory creatures that will have a go at this guy … you think about those types of things when you're designing a creature?

Absolutely. Even if it's something I'll never design or we might not see. One thing I notice that a lot of people do – and it's not bad, but it's something I didn't want to do right from the beginning – is an alpha predator, like a great white shark. It's fun to design a creature like that, but to me it's a little more interesting to do something a bit further down the food chain because it gives me more options.

Q: Looking at your color renders, when you got to them, were you thinking about whether it was a male or a female or where you still trying to nail down its general form?

A little bit of both. I was trying at this point to think about color a bit more, and that does make you think about whether it's a male or female. I still didn't know that right until the very end. With this color test, the main thing I was trying to discover was color, and then just seeing how these characters looked in a more finished state and what needed to change. If you look at the first Rhinodino I did, it's very close to the final one, but there are still simple textural and color things that changed. Doing this color exploration really helped me to realize that.

Q: Did you think about this creature having fur, or were you always thinking it was going to have heavy skin?

I always knew I wanted to have heavy skin on this for one reason – if I did a male I wanted to do a really bold mane

These sketches were done in a small sketchbook. I try to carry at least one sketchbook with me at all times, in case inspiration strikes. I sketch and write down ideas so I can explore a design as much as possible.

11

around its chest or its back, or even something on its tail, with bright-red fibery hair, almost like a rooster. I wanted to do a very bold statement, so this creature would not only have this massive bony formation on its head but also a really colorful mane. So, what we have here is probably the design for the female.

Q: Talk a bit more about how he eats.

This creature does not roam around its environment looking to eat whatever is in its path … it's not hunting for the sake of hunting, it's eating for the sake of eating.

Q: Does it flee or fight, as prey?

I imagine it uses the tool on its head to defend itself as well as smash up rocks and mounds to get at its food. This is a herd animal, so when it's under attack the females create a circle around the babies, protecting them. Seventy-five percent of its body is its front legs, so it could withstand being attacked from the front. But if a large creature got behind it and took its legs out, it would be toast. I watched a documentary on wildebeest,

and they do something called 'mobbing' – if one wildebeest is being picked on by a lion or something, the other wildebeest turn around and just charge at the lion. This creature can also use its front legs to charge.

Q: During the process, did you get really stuck at any point and, if so, how did you work through that?

For me the difficult question was how it's going to eat. I knew how it would go about finding its food but how it got it into its mouth was really difficult to work out. I was wondering how it would actually get to its food, it's like a dog with one of those collars on. I did have the long tongue early on but I forgot about it. I was looking at stuff on Pinterest and came across the diagram of the hummingbird skull and how its tongue works, and it filled in that extra 20 percent I was looking for. Who would have thought I would use a picture of a hummingbird to design a creature like this? I found that piece of reference to be pretty critical in terms of not only bringing something new to the piece but also fixing a functionality problem with how the creature eats.

Above: Some of the sketches blocked out in ZBrush. I work with a dark material to help me focus on a character's silhouette.

Left: Photographs I took at the LA Zoo and the Natural History Museum to use as reference for the Rhinodino. In the bottom three images, you can see the incredibly helpful rhinoceros who posed beautifully for the photo session!

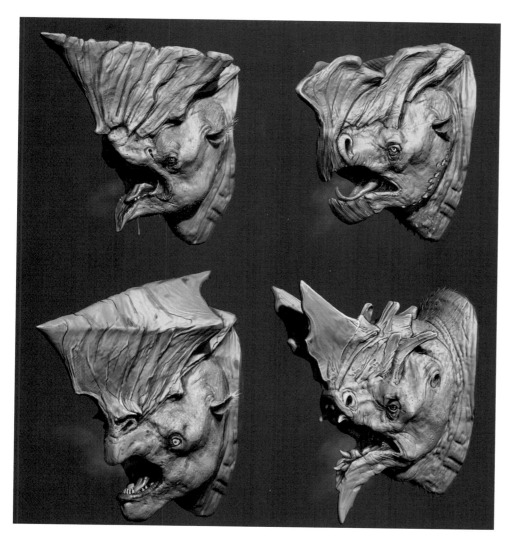

Left: I explored different design paths for the head. I wanted to create options for the bony mass on the creature's head and also for the shapes of the eyes, ears and mouth.

Below: I tested color and material platelets out before focusing on the entire figure.

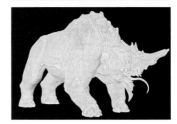

↑ Above: The final sculpt posed and ready for Polypaint.

↖ Opposite page top: There is something I really enjoy about this design. I don't think it was the right path for the Rhinodino but I think it had some interesting design elements, like the plow-shaped protrusions and beak.

➔ Right column: These materials were rendered out of ZBrush and used to create color variation, cavity maps, specular values and lighting scenarios that were used in the final image.

egg thief

BRYAN WYNIA

Q: What was your end goal when you were coming up with this creature?

This creature was totally blue sky (something from nothing). I was not sure what I wanted to move on to after the Rhinodino, so for the speed sculpt I grabbed a head off of a creature I did about a year ago to see what I could morph that into. Then I let happy accidents happen to see where they would take me. There was not really much of an end goal other than trying to find something that worked.

Q: Did you use Creature Matrix at all or was it totally blue sky?

Yeah, it was totally blue sky, no Creature Matrix, no creature description. Really just sketching to find a creature or a character.

Q: While you were sketching, what kind of inspiration/s did you come across?

When I was doing the speed sculpt, I was trying to come up with different options. So there is one that looks a bit like a wolf and there's one that looks like a hairless mole rat. Then I was referencing small mammals, primate-looking things. The last one I did was the guy with the beak, and it went from there. I then took the speed sculpts and painted on top of them to make some thumbnails and try to find out more about the characters.

Q: Did you do some pencil sketches for them?

No pencil sketches just speed sculpts, and then right into the paint-over thumbnails.

Q: How do you start when you are creating a blue sky kind of character?

I came home one day after I took my family to the Natural History Museum. I saw a skull for big wolf or something like that and I used that as inspiration. When I'm doing thumbnails or different speed sculpts for one character, I like to explore as many ideas as possible. So the only rule I

have with the speed sculpts is to try to do something fairly different from the one I did just before it.

Q: How many variations did you do?

I did a total of six, and then, based on the feedback from other artists in this book, I picked two.

Q: How do you imagine your creature moves or sounds? Did this influence how you developed it?

The story I came up with for the character was that it is an egg thief. I pictured this character as primate-like, a small mammal or a sloth or something that creeps around in the trees and is very opportunistic. When it sees an open nest, no matter what kind of eggs are in it, it sneaks in and grabs some food for itself.

Q: Is this your normal process that you go through when you are creating creatures, or is this something unusual that you've never tried before?

This is a pretty typical process for personal work. Most of the time for a film or a game, you have a pretty set idea of what the character is going to be like – there is a character description – but for blue sky creature design, whether that is personal or very early on in a project, this is pretty close to how I work.

Q: Did you consider variations as far as male, female or babies?

I didn't do male/female variations but I did other variations. For example, one has a good deal of hair and has a bit of a fantasy vibe to it, while another variation has vulture influences and hair that is more sporadic on the head and coarser, thicker and wiry, and it also has weird fleshy appendages coming off the top of its head.

Continued on page 22…

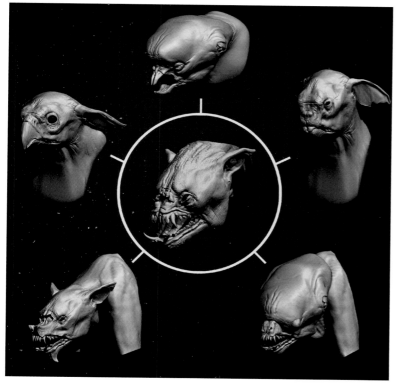

Above: A resign cast of a turkey head. Using casts as reference is an invaluable source of information.

Top left: You can find reference everywhere! While preparing Thanksgiving last year, I saw an opportunity to gather some inspiration from the turkey. The textures and color are a gold mine for a creature designer.

Left: The original mesh in the middle was used to create all of these new ideas. You can see how many variations one mesh can create.

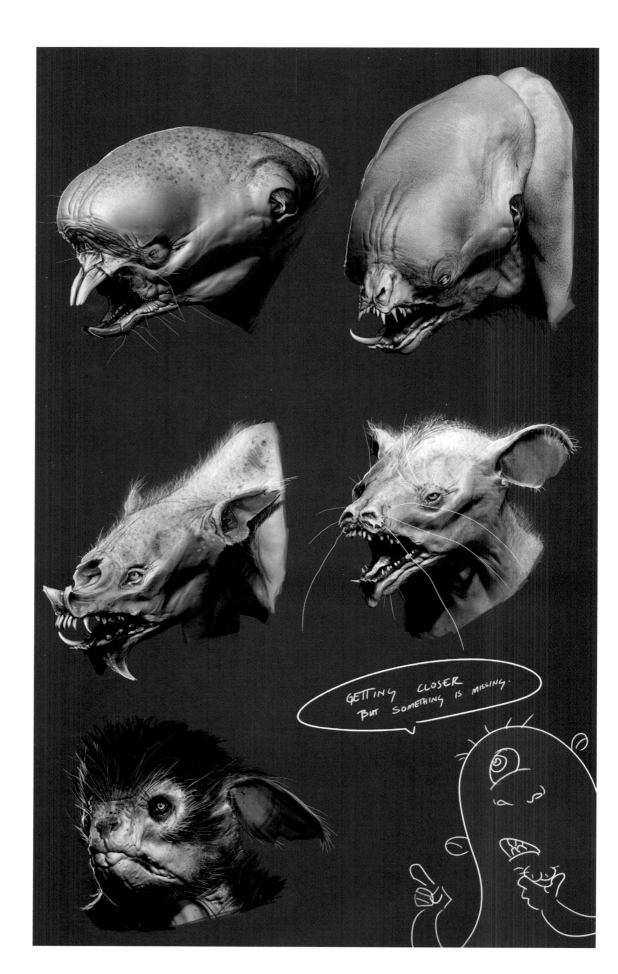

During the creation of this book, I started drawing this weird cyclops creature who always seemed to have something to say. This is what late-night monster-making sessions create. I fear he now lives in my attic and eats burritos.

⬆ This page: Using feedback from the cyclops and the other artists, I decided to move forward with these designs. I explored some ideas of color with a quick wash in Photoshop.

Continued from page 18…

Q: **What did you try in terms of other markings on the beak or giving it teeth, for example?**

I knew I wanted to give this creature hair and not feathers, which would make it look like a bipedal bird. So I tried looking at different types of hair. In terms of markings, in the early color sketches you can see I have used just red to black so it had some sort of character to it. In the end when this guy was developing into the egg thief, I took away those flashy colors because this creature wouldn't have a bright-red hair pattern as it's trying to sneak into the trees to steal eggs.

Q: **It looks like you didn't experiment too much with a lot of colors, that you wanted to stay with more fleshy tones…**

I knew I wanted it to be in a flesh tone. I didn't get too crazy with markings or anything like that because it already has lots of areas of interest – big ears, hair, a beak, and the egg-dissolving sack (which we can talk about later). I thought that if I went crazy with the markings as well it would feel like I had gotten too busy with the character.

Q: **During the process, did you get stuck at all or was it pretty smooth?**

It was a fairly smooth process for the most part. I did debate whether to paint or sculpt the hair, but since I knew I was not going to be printing it I thought it would be faster to paint it.

Q: **Tell us about the egg sack …**

When I was working on the character I asked myself the question, "How does it eat the eggs it steals?" One idea I had was that its beak crushes the eggs, almost like a can opener, and it would then swallow down the embryo. But I thought that crushing eggs would be very loud, which would not be good for a creature that sneaks into a nest to steal eggs. So instead I imagined it swallowing the eggs whole. The way its beak is structured means it can lean over the nest, grab an egg and swallow it. Its mouth extends even beyond the beak so it has a pretty wide range of motion. Then, the wattle or the sack in the neck is its first digestive track. The egg slides down there, where it dissolves and softens up and then it slides down into its stomach, the second part of the digestive track, where the egg is digested fully.

Q: **At the very end you had two variations. Which one did you finish first and how did you go about making the variations?**

I finished the one with the hair and the little feelers, with a kind of purple feel to the image. Then I thought I would do a variation so I could speak about that process because that is something that I do quite a bit on most projects. I tried to do something similar yet fairly different. I wanted to do something pretty different with the hair … I grabbed the Liquify tool in Photoshop, moved a few things around, and tried to infuse a little bit more vulture into this one and give it a real dirt bag vibe that you would expect from something that steals lots of unhatched eggs and swallows them whole. This guy is not really the most noble of creatures.

Q: **In looking at your sculpting process, at one point it looks like you were playing with a longer beak but then you went back to the shorter one. What made you go back to the shorter beak?**

Once again, I felt like he already had a lot of areas of interest, including the egg-dissolving sack, so I didn't want him to be too noisy. Also, I didn't want him to be an alpha predator with all the best tools. I picked only a few tools for him so he doesn't have the best of every weapon … he still has some vulnerabilities. This creature is probably pretty far down the food chain. I was trying to 'listen' to my character as I was sculpting it – to the rhythms in the forms and also the rhythms of the proportions of the character.

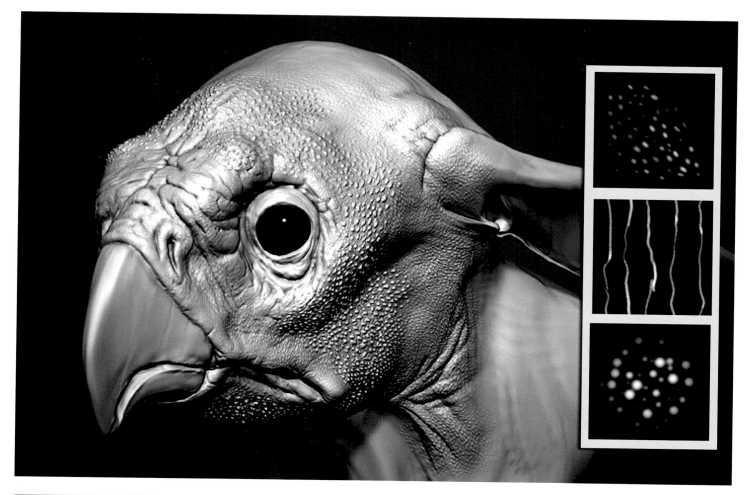

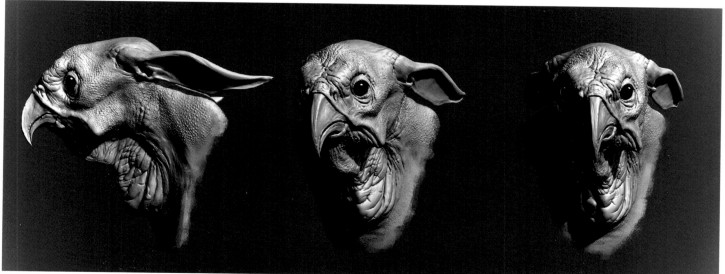

⬆ This page: Using alphas, I created an interesting texture
for the creature's skin. I referred to my reference images to
inform me how the skin might look.

 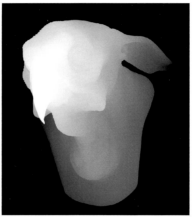  

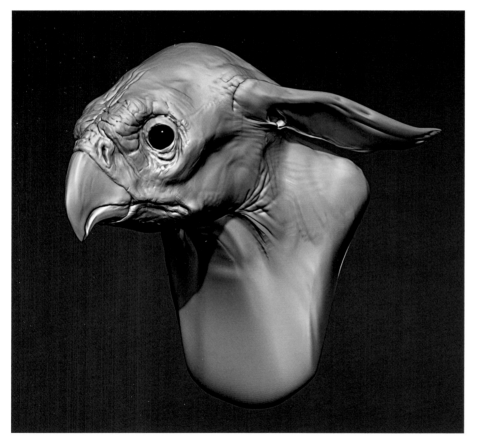 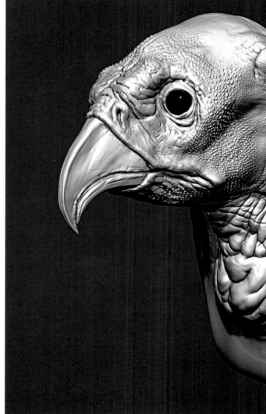

⬆ Top row: The render pass used for creating the final image. You will notice a bright-red image with a blue section for the eye; this render is used as a mask and for making quick selections inside Photoshop.

⬆ Above row: You can see how the design evolved from the speed sculpt to the final design.

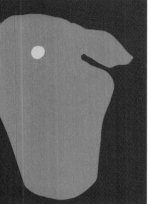
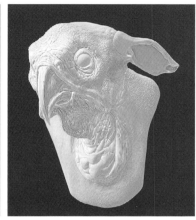

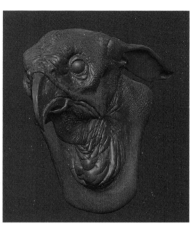

 The final image – alternate version.

⬆ The final image.

bog bomber

BRYAN WYNIA

Q: What was your end goal when you started thinking about this creature?

I wanted to create a predatorial, aquatic creature.

Q: Did you use the Creature Matrix for this creature? If not, where did your inspiration come from?

I didn't look at the matrix for this creature. I was on vacation in Eugene, Oregon, with my family when the inspiration hit me. We took a drive out to the coast … that part of Oregon's landscape is pretty inspiring … driving back from the coast I saw these massive trees full of branches, literally from about two feet to the top full of branches. Some of the trees were dead or not very full of vegetation, but they had masses of moss growing out of them. I saw one tree, fallen over into the lake, with branches covering the entire length of it. Seeing the branches floating on top of the lake instantly reminded me of an alligator mixed with a water mine. I thought that'd be a cool creature. Luckily I had one of my sketchbooks with me so I was able to write down some notes (see image opposite).

Q: When you are faced with a blank page, what goes through your mind – how do you start?

Once I had that initial inspiration, I started to explore the water mine concept a little bit more. I started thinking about a creature almost like an alligator, something floating on the surface of the water or buried under the sand. Then when I started my sketches I started to narrow it down and do some problem-solving. From the initial thought process I started bouncing ideas off of my own head or with Ian, James and Josh (also artists in this book). Spit-balling ideas like this is a good way to see what sticks and what doesn't.

Q: How do you imagine your creature moves and sounds? Did this influence how you developed it?

I imagine this creature has a manatee meets alligator body shape. It has long sensors … I don't really want to call them antenna … coming off its body. The initial inspiration was the tree coming out of the water, but I also looked at some sea urchins and some reptiles.

I imagined that this creature floats in the water, and, as other creatures come by and touch it, its sensors (it doesn't have eyes) go off in response, and then it pounces on its prey. I also imagined that, like a shark's nose can pick up electronic signals, it can sense body heat … maybe there is a temperature regulator inside those sensors so that when a fish comes by it can sense the temperature or maybe the vibrations from the creature it preys upon.

I also imagined that its tail is like an anchor and it can take on air and be buoyant, which allows it to swim, or it can expel the air and sink to the bottom, like a submarine. Another idea I had was that it can use its tail to burrow into the riverbank and embed itself there, or use it like a prehensile tail and wrap it around things. I looked at actual boat anchors as references when I designed the silhouette for the tail's shape.

Q: How many variations did you do and what direction did you go in to achieve the end result?

From my sketches, I did a good few variations. I did some that were of a traditional alligator mixed with some kind of fish and with other aquatic elements. I did one sketch when I was thinking about a manatee with front arms and a strong, massive back tail. In the end I didn't go with hands but with kind of giant forks or hooks that it would use to pin food.

Q: Was this a normal or unusual design process for you?

This is a pretty straightforward example of how I normally design, where something just bit me with inspiration and I did a few sketches to do problem-solving before I got into 3D and started to build the design. I let it evolve in 3D … I didn't hang on to the sketch.

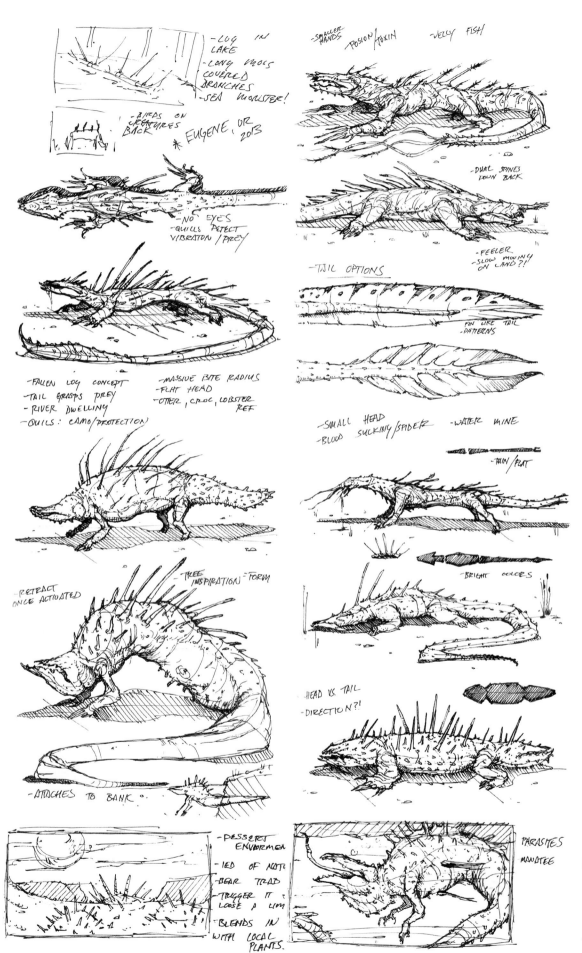

-LOG IN LAKE
-LONG MOSS COVERED BRANCHES
-SEA MONSTER!
-BIRDS ON CREATURES BACK
★ EUGENE, OR 2013

-SMALLER HANDS   POSION/TOXIN   -JELLY FISH

-NO EYES
-QUILLS DETECT VIBRATION/PREY

-DUAL SPINES DOWN BACK

-FEELER
-SLOW MOVING ON LAND?!

-TAIL OPTIONS

-FIN LIKE TAIL
-PATTERNS

-FALLEN LOG CONCEPT
-TAIL GRASPS PREY
-RIVER DWELLING
-QUILS: CAMO/PROTECTION

-MASSIVE BITE RADIUS
-FLAT HEAD
-OTTER, CROC, LOBSTER REF

-SMALL HEAD
-BLOOD SUCKING/SPIDER   -WATER MINE

-THIN/FLAT

-RETRACT ONCE ACTIVATED

-TREE INSPIRATION FORM

-BRIGHT COLORS

-ATTACHES TO BANK.

-HEAD VS. TAIL
-DIRECTION?!

-DESSERT ENVIRMOEN
-IED OF NOTE
-BEAR TRAD
-TRIGGER IT LOOSE A LIM
-BLENDS IN WITH LOCAL PLANTS.

PARASITES
MANATEE

◄ Here you can see the various design options I explored in my sketches. On the top left you can also see the quick note I wrote about my inspiration for this creature, the trees in Oregon.

29

Q: **What ideas did you have for it to stalk its prey?**

It would be floating in the water, very murky water, similar to the illustration, and once a creature was sensed, it would pounce on it. One piece of inspiration I got was an image of a guy with a pet sea turtle that is fed mice. The sea turtle just devoured the mouse and used its claw to hook the mouse like a fork; he then bit one half and pulled his head and hand away from each other and just snapped this guy right in half. It was a pretty powerful image to see, and it gave me a lot of inspiration about how this guy would hunt. You can see that inspiration in the final illustration with what I did with Josh's Red-finned Slark.

I went through lots of different ideas. I think there is one sketch where you can see this creature is in the desert. At one point I was going to have this thing hunt my first creature, the Rhinodino. If the Rhinodino stepped on it, one of the sensors coming out of the ground would quickly inject the Rhinodino with a toxin, which by itself isn't dangerous but once it goes into the bloodstream and mixes with the blood of the Rhinodino, it becomes an explosive, just like a landmine. So the Rhinodino would step on it, take a few more steps, and then there would be a small explosion that would blow its leg off and it would die from blood loss. Then this creature would unearth itself and come out and eat it.

But in the end, I wanted to stick to the original inspiration, which was the log in the water, and I thought it would be a good opportunity to do something different from the other creatures I had done, by doing an aquatic creature.

Q: **Did you consider making variations – male, female, old, babies?**

I didn't really do any design exploration. If I had to tell you right now whether this is a male or female, this would be a male, and I would see it acting very much like a male alligator that is hanging around just to create offspring. I don't see this creature as being a very nurturing animal; it's pretty primal in that its job is to eat and to hunt – and it does this pretty effectively. As far as reproducing, it would not be the most graceful thing or the most nurturing parent.

Q: **At any point in the process did you get stuck, and, if so, how did you resolve this?**

I wasn't really sure how to move forward with the hands at one point, so I did a set of quick sketches and thumbnails to come up with different options. The same goes for when the mouth was open, because I wanted to show how it functions. So I just tried to explore different ideas. For the mouth, I looked at the sarcastic fringehead fish, which has a mouth similar to the Predator with extra flaps that open wide and make it look very aggressive. But I felt like that was a little expected.

There was another drawing I did where it had two sets of jaws – one interior and one exterior. Eels are similar to this, as is the classic design of the alien, where one jaw is for grabbing and one is for tearing. When I was at the museum in Australia I found this skeletal structure of the mouth of a blue groper fish, which has plates in the back of its mouth that I assume are for grinding food. I thought they made a really cool and interesting shape, so in my thumbnails I explored that design and did something similar with this creature.

Q: **You found a lot of inspiration for this creature in different areas. Can you tell us a little more about that?**

Like I said, I had the image of the log and the lake from my trip as the initial inspiration, but I also wanted to pull inspiration from some areas that weren't so typical. In my reference images there are some photos of reptiles that I came in contact with when I was on a trip to Adelaide in Australia. The picture of the blue groper mouth is from the museum in Adelaide. I referenced some pictures of rock textures and a picture I took of a sea urchin in New Zealand.

The other thing I started to do for inspiration was to pull from actual memories and experiences that I have had. This was something a little new for me, but I think it's something all artists do, possibly unintentionally. Having those life experiences and not always sitting in front of the computer I think are really important – to be able to pull on them and use them to inform your design choices when you're creating a creature. You're creating something fantastical or something make-believe, but you're wanting it to have a sense of familiarity so when the

viewer sees it there's something about it that reminds them of something they've seen before. It's something totally new that they haven't seen before but it's not so far-fetched that they don't know what they're looking at. So those experiences are definitely a feature I tried to pull on when designing this creature.

This page: A collection of reference photographs and inspiration from my travels: reptiles from Australia, sea life from New Zealand, and trees from the Oregon coast.

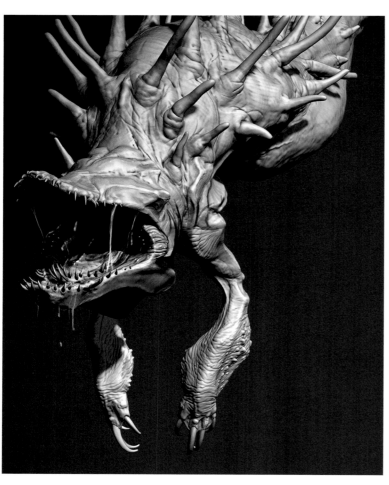

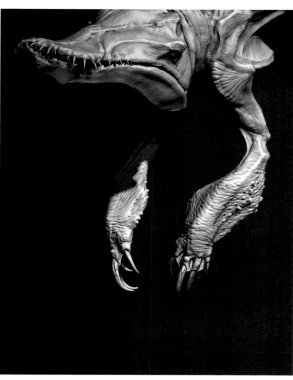
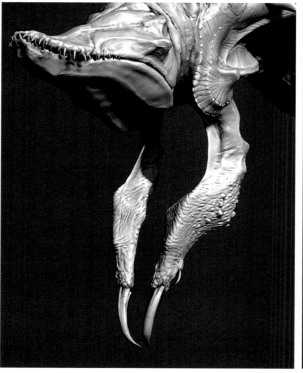

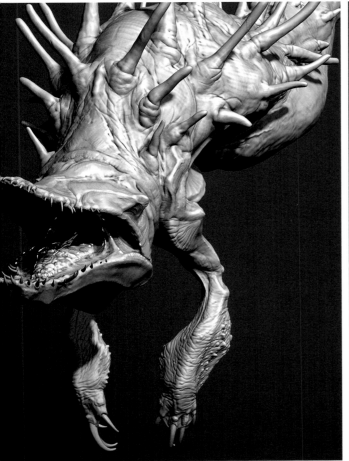

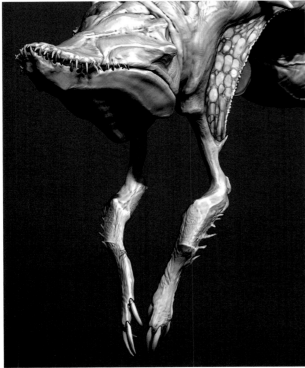

↑ Top row: I blocked out some different design options for the mouth and painted over them to see what direction best fit the character.

↑ Above row: Applying the same method, I explored options for his hands and how he might move and capture his prey.

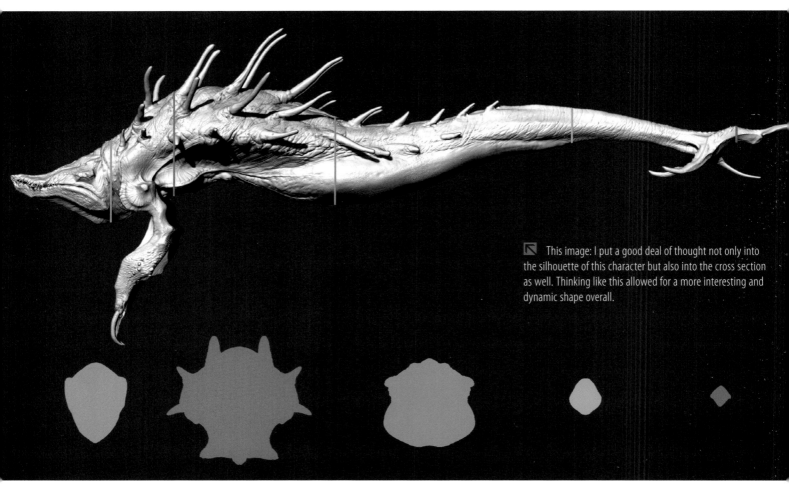

This image: I put a good deal of thought not only into the silhouette of this character but also into the cross section as well. Thinking like this allowed for a more interesting and dynamic shape overall.

Right images: The creature did not have much break-up as far as material goes. For example, he does not have a bony protrusion or hair. So, I used textures and various forms to try to get as much material break-up and variation to the creature as possible.

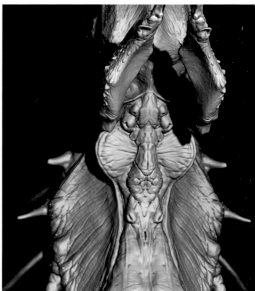

This page: The final sculpt seen from multiple views. Note the subtle gesture introduced to all of the forms.

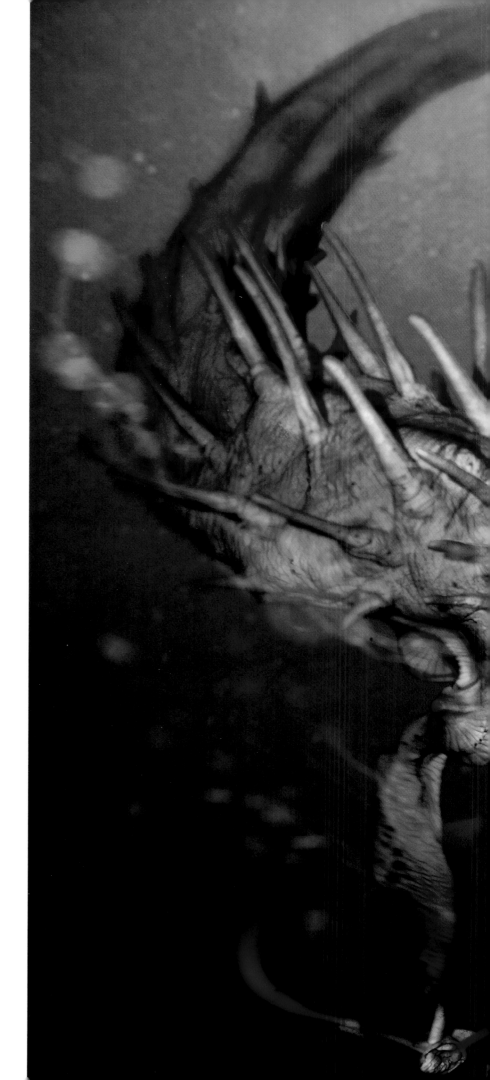

This Red-finned Slark has triggered the Bog Bomber and looks to have suffered a bit of a flesh wound!

other concepts

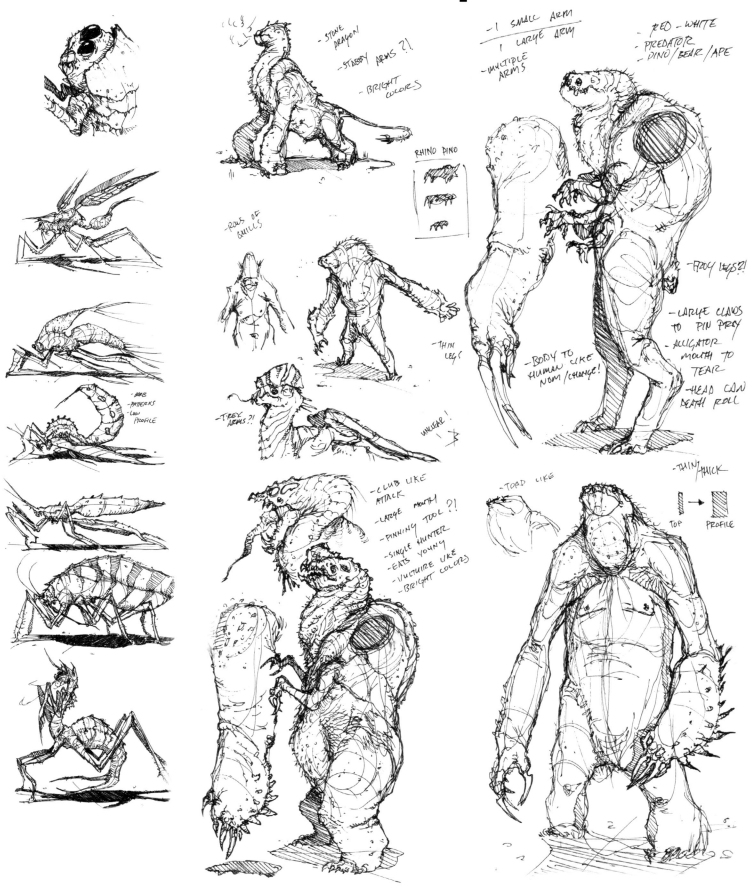

- STONE DRAGON
- STABBY ARMS ?!
- BRIGHT COLORS

- 1 SMALL ARM
- 1 LARGE ARM
- MULTIPLE ARMS

- RED - WHITE
- PREDATOR
- DINO / BEAR / APE

RHINO PINO

- ROWS OF QUILLS

- THIN LEGS

- BODY TO HUMAN LIKE NORM / CHANGE!

- T-REX ARMS ?!

UNCLEAR !

- FROG LEGS?!

- LARGE CLAWS TO PIN PREY
- ALLIGATOR MOUTH TO TEAR
- HEAD CAN DEATH ROLL

- BUG PATTERNS
- LOW PROFILE

- CLUB LIKE ATTACK
- LARGE MOUTH
- PINNING TOOL ?!
- SINGLE HUNTER
- EATS YOUNG
- VULTURE LIKE
- BRIGHT COLORS

- TOAD LIKE

- THIN / THICK

TOP → PROFILE

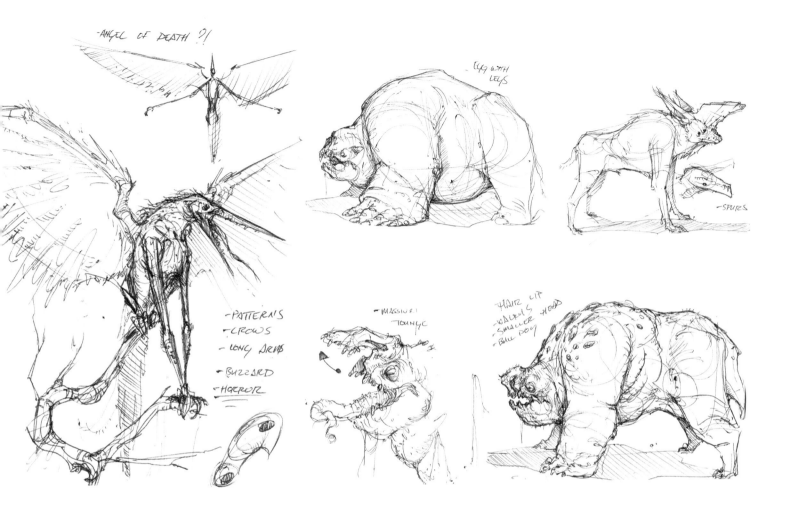

- ANGEL OF DEATH ?!
- EGG WITH LEGS
- MASSIVE! TOUNGE
- SPURS
- HAIR LIP
- WALRUS HEAD
- SMALLER HEAD
- BULL DOG
- PATTERN'S
- CROWS
- LONG ARMS
- BUZZARD
- HORROR

These sketches, speed sculpts and designs are ideas that didn't make it past the early ideation stage, but present exciting would-be creatures and concepts to explore in the future.

Skunk Ape

39

andrew baker

BIOGRAPHY

I remember watching my father, a painter, create a portrait of an Arab man. My young mind questioned how those brush marks created that realistic-looking man on the canvas. Since then, I've been trying to answer that question by making marks of my own. My father was my first mentor, and he means the world to me. He is my inspiration for what a man should be. Wayne Barlowe has been another big influence on me, and, after meeting him a few years back, I like to think of him as a mentor not only for his design genius but also for his attitude towards this tough industry and his demeanor, which is humbling and something I strive to achieve.

Working extremely hard was definitely what got me where I am today. I studied design at university but it wasn't solely what got me the jobs that led me to work at Weta. I spent a lot of time working on my own, trying many different programs to learn how to be a commercial artist. I felt this was the only path to a creative job because working as a fine artist seemed impossible. I was lucky enough to be studying in New Zealand at the time, and one of the first places I sent my reel to was Weta. It would only be a year later that I got a job working on *The Adventures of Tintin* doing digital sets. During that time I worked really hard on my digital sculpting portfolio and then got a job as a Creature Designer at Weta Workshop, where I have been ever since and now work as a Senior Designer.

At Weta, my day typically is supposed to start around 8 am, but generally the design creatures roll in around 9 am … Tsk tsk! Then I spend my 12-hour day working on a wide variety of projects, after which I go home to play with my dog and work late into the night on any other projects I have on the go. Outside of work, I love to do photography, especially macro photography of insects. I'm also a musician going on 17 years now, playing guitar mainly, and have broken out onto the banjo in the last few months.

My advice for young artists: Work hard, work smart. Don't be concerned with what other artists are doing; find what you love to do and do it hard! Never lose site that storytelling is the most important aspect of creating art. In this industry the biggest challenges to an artist are competition and staying fresh. It's hard to be noticed, especially with software now giving so many a platform to perform on. I think now more than anything a unique idea and a story will separate you from the pack.

In my future I see robots, lots of robots. Oh, and flying cars.

kha-philian peasant

ANDREW BAKER

Q: Where did your inspiration for this creature come from?

The idea for this organ-grinding, hooka-smoking alien came from a study I was doing of a microscopic water flea, *Daphnia pulex*. These tiny creatures have some fantastic alien forms and such a bizarre personality to them. The original drawing and studies I did were a little too ominous, and I wanted to create a piece that had more character to it. I wanted to give it some humor of its own that relates to our world but sits entirely in its own.

I've always been a huge fan of Wayne Barlowe's work, and one of his pieces, the *Vasparian Minstrel*, in particular was a big inspiration for this piece. Often people choose to depict a warrior, a villain or a giant creature as an illustration of a world. But I love those smaller moments that are more passer-by moments. We've all had them, especially anyone who's traveled, where you come across some vagabond shuffling along with his cart or a busker oozing with character playing jazz for money … these are the little slices of life that give you another perspective on the world we are familiar with.

For alien worlds, I love seeing this side of life and asking myself what the streets would look and smell like, and what the life outside of all the action would be like when the cameras aren't filming. These notes to a culture really fill a world for me, and I wanted to capture one of those moments in this piece.

This guy is just sitting, playing his little organ grinder, possibly for his own amusement or maybe to collect some kind of charity from people passing by. The smoking is something that might be keeping him there, just a habit to pass the time, who knows? I just like the idea that creatures can do more than fight, hunt or be 'badass', but can enjoy sitting down, cranking some music and smoking the occasional pipe, even if it is on a grotty street somewhere.

Q: Tell us a bit more about the creature.

His make-up, while looking somewhat complex, is rather a simple biological construct. A large, carapace-like husk covers the back of this creature like a cloak or robe. Hidden inside is his abstract torso with a flexible exoskeleton-like structure (unlike any we've encountered on Earth) consisting of cartilage and soft muscle tissue. His limbs end in leathery arm-like appendages with tentacle-like fingers. There appears to be no skeletal structure inside the limbs and they seem to grip things quite delicately, allowing the creature to play instruments, sew, smoke pipes and the like.

This is a very lazy creature. They have become lazy through evolution, as they no longer need to pursue their food because they can get it from a store or buy it from a vendor. They used to solely feed on smaller insects; those leathery appendages were originally used to catch the insects. In this study we can see a few stray bugs floating around the creature's head; these bugs are more of a nuisance nowadays rather than a vital food source, although they do provide a sufficient snack every now and again. Generally, though, these creatures prefer to eat noodles.

Due to their lazy nature, they're not often found farming on the lands or doing hard work of any sort. They tend to run corporations or get into politics. Otherwise they sponge off where they can and get by through resorting to petty fraud crimes if need be. Not a trustworthy species in my books!

Q: How did you create this creature?

I created this guy in ZBrush and did the concept in 3D straight away. I had already done some studies of *Daphnia pulex,* and I had the idea of his body when going into it. I rendered all my layers from ZBrush with a multitude of shaders and my BPR passes as well. Once I get my layers composed in Photoshop, I spend a fair bit of time painting into my pieces, creating atmospheres and bringing the details up through some brush work. I rarely like to use photos in artwork except for texture. I enjoy painting over the renders and giving my pieces a painterly finish. Although this process means for slightly more work, it gives me a nice control over everything. You can lose this control when you're overlaying images to get your artwork to the

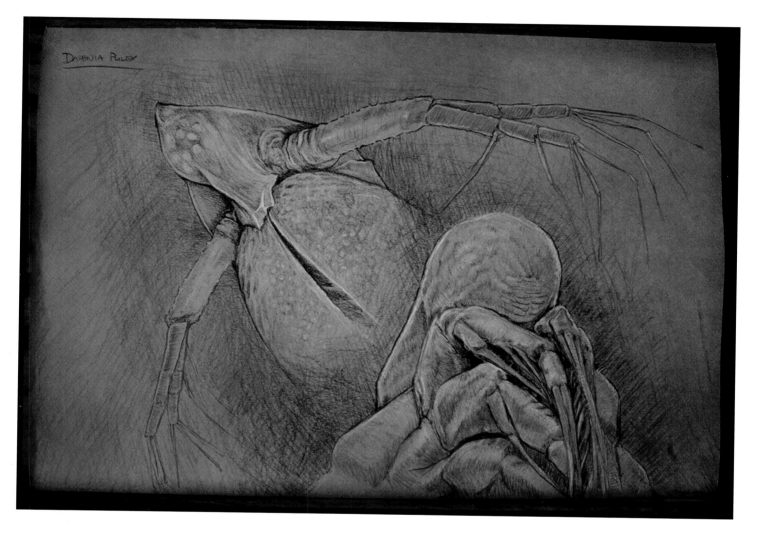

A drawing done for research into *Daphnia pulex*, a microscopic water flea.

finish line. I thoroughly enjoyed working this guy up.
I always love the fact that doing it in ZBrush means I get a
sculpt as well as an illustration out of the work. I decided
to do some renders in Maya to show the overall forms of
the creature. I decimated the mesh from ZBrush, and, using
mental ray and Maya, I created a resin-like material with
the SSS shader and did a very basic final gather render to
composite in Photoshop.

→ Right: A silhouette study of the Kha-philian species with its legs down.

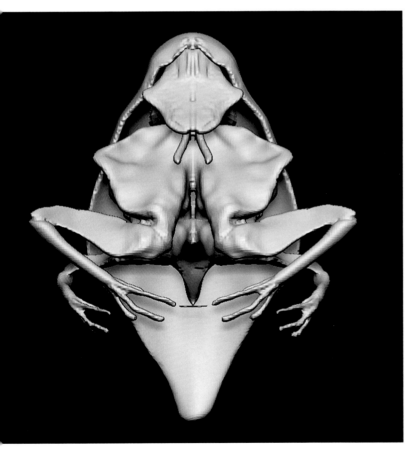

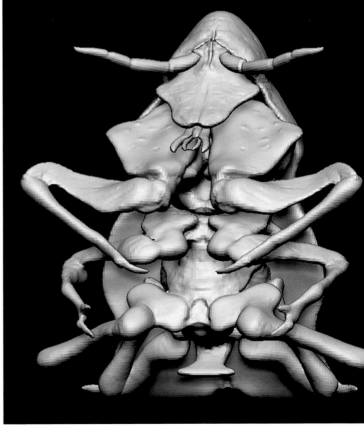

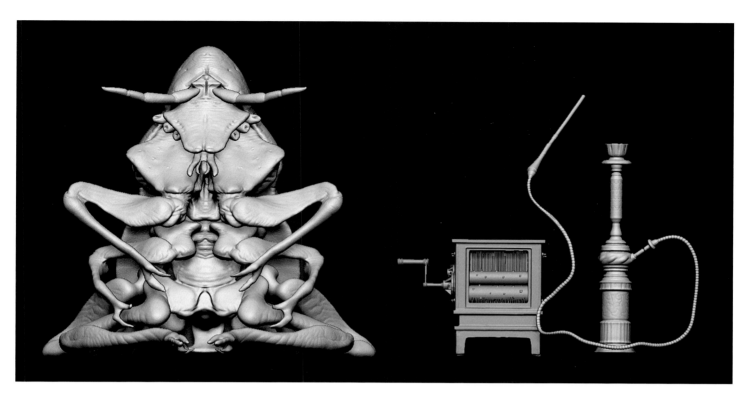

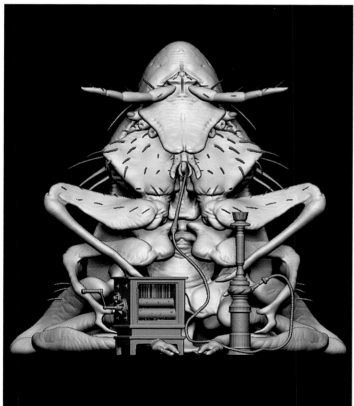

This page and opposite page bottom images: Some of the sculpting stages. I used DynaMesh a lot to constantly judge how the overall silhouette was affecting and adding geometry as I needed. I was also building the creature's assets, the organ grinder and hooka pipe, on separate sub-tools.

This page: Having decimated the sculpt in ZBrush, I brought it into Maya to do some renders to show the form better.

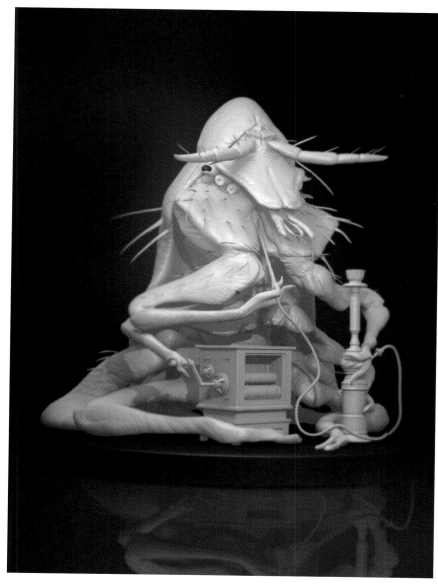

↖ Left: A single frame from Maya showing just the form details.

↓ Below images: Some of the renders from ZBrush that I used in Photoshoip to begin layering up the final illustration.

↑ This page: The final passes of the illustration in Photoshop. At this stage I started adding more paint techniques and overlaid some noise from photographed textures, like moss or metal.

→ Opposite page: The finished Kha-philian Peasant.

geilo

Q: What was your idea with this creature?

The idea behind this creature came from thinking about the military industrial complex, and all the sorts of black ops that go on there as far as genetic experimentation. Hence the name of this creature: GEILO – Genetically Engineered, Intelligent, Lethal Organism. These creatures were designed for killing, in a number of manners. Whether they are needed for soldiering or assassinations, they have the ability to be quiet, quick and brutal.

Q: What inspired you in creating this creature?

Jamie Beswarick's alien designs have always been a huge inspiration for me on this subject matter. I wanted to create something that had no compassion whatsoever. They were intentionally designed to follow orders, but, unless the creatures' designers used some sort of artificial programming, they could not make the creatures intelligent enough to follow simple orders. Therefore, brain development had to be high. I like the idea that with all this manipulation that has gone into developing the creatures, it somehow backfires and the scientists responsible for this Frankenstein-like creation end up paying the price.

Q: Tell us about the creature's anatomy.

The design for the creature had to be bipedal – they had to be able to carry a weapon and carry out basic tasks. But they didn't need human hands or delicate hands as they were never intended to create things with their hands, only destroy things. They are fed mainly protein and have metabolisms like a carnivore, although, unlike most cats, stamina is not a problem for them.

They have an extremely flexible skeleton surrounded by an artificial muscle system, which creates the ribbed effect over their skin, giving it a panel-like look. This creates a lot more flexibility for this creature to be able to extend the reach in its arms and legs as well as its neck, making his punches lethal – they are able to explode a concrete wall with a single punch. They also have two sets of eyes – one set are binocular, much like ours, and the second have

heat-seeking and infrared capabilities, allowing it to see in the dark. The scientists who developed this creature were very creative with their skin colors and based this guy on a poisonous dart frog, but they also had planned to make a range of different colors specific to their task.

The production of GEILOs have been halted and the first prototypes are at large. The live a tragic existence with their beak-like mouth rendering them unable to communicate effectively through language, but they are believed to have developed some sort of communication and are proving very difficult to track. All that is left is a trail of destruction and a lot of missing persons.

Q: Did you start with any sketches for this creature?

For these pieces I again used ZBrush and Photoshop. I didn't start with any drawings as I had a pretty good idea of what I wanted this guy to look like, so I dove straight into ZBrush. I normally do this for concept work with creatures, as I find 3D a good way to resolve designs.

I used DynaMesh extensively for this sculpt and also did a Polypaint directly onto the sculpt. This saved me having to paint in the coloration in the final piece. I rendered out multiple shaders and layers from ZBrush, which gave me lots to play with in Photoshop. Once layered and blended, I decided to change the composition somewhat, thinking that a straight up-and-down shot was looking a little boring. So I put it on a bit of a Dutch angle, creating the perspective of the viewer potentially being another victim.

I didn't want to spend a lot of time on the background, so I kept it fairly simple, with the subjects the main focus. As with most pieces, I wanted to add a sense of atmosphere … I used a large airbrush to knock back and bring forward certain areas. Once I got all of my painting done, I flattened the whole image to apply some post-processing. Using a color filter, I applied a purple layer over the whole image with a Lighten Blend mode, which gives the shadows a bit more life. I put a filter of noise over it for a consistent finish. After that, I called it done.

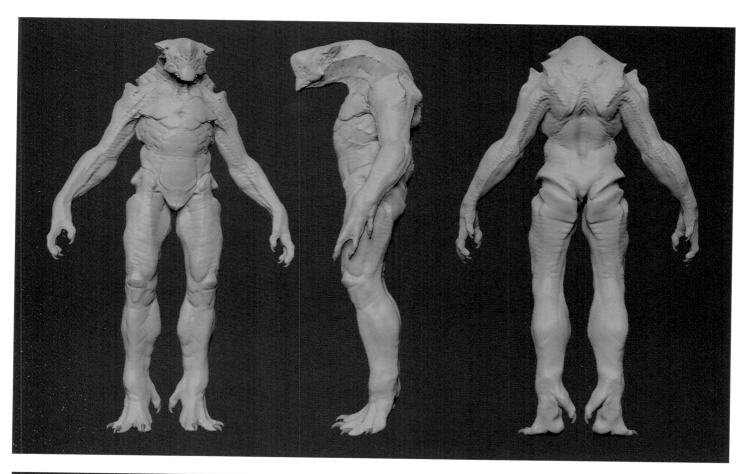

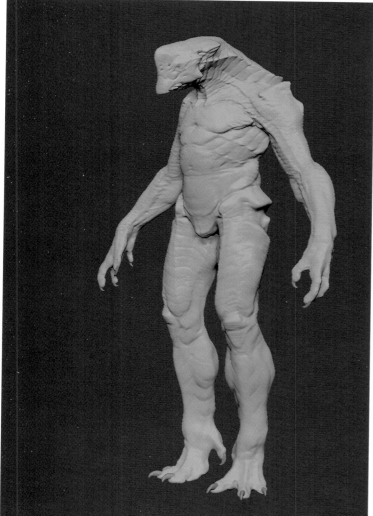

This page: Some early sculpting in ZBrush to get the ribbed skin feel.

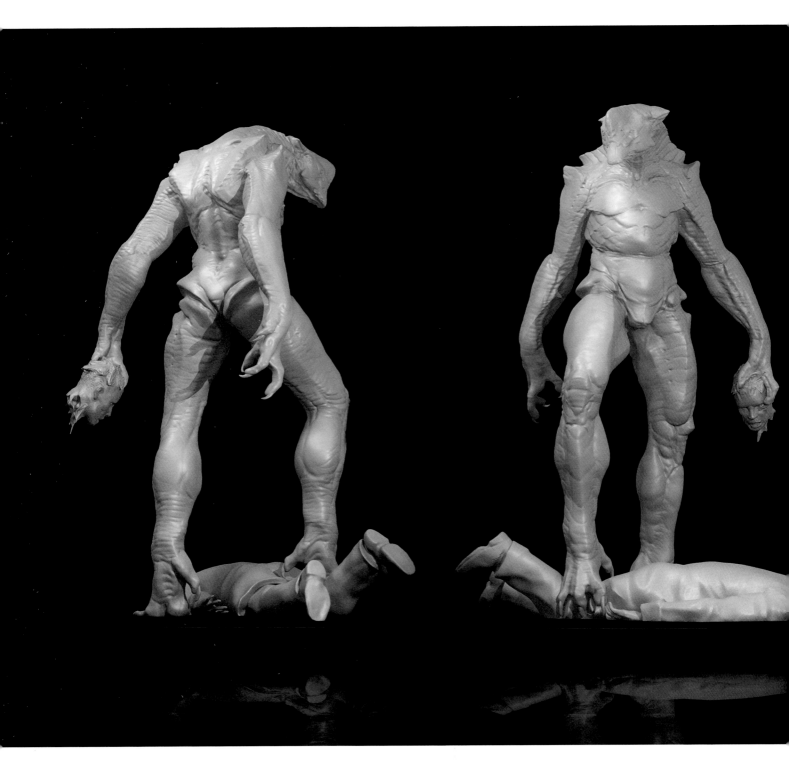

↑ Maya render done in mental ray to show off the creature's forms.

GE-ILO #0001 : \\

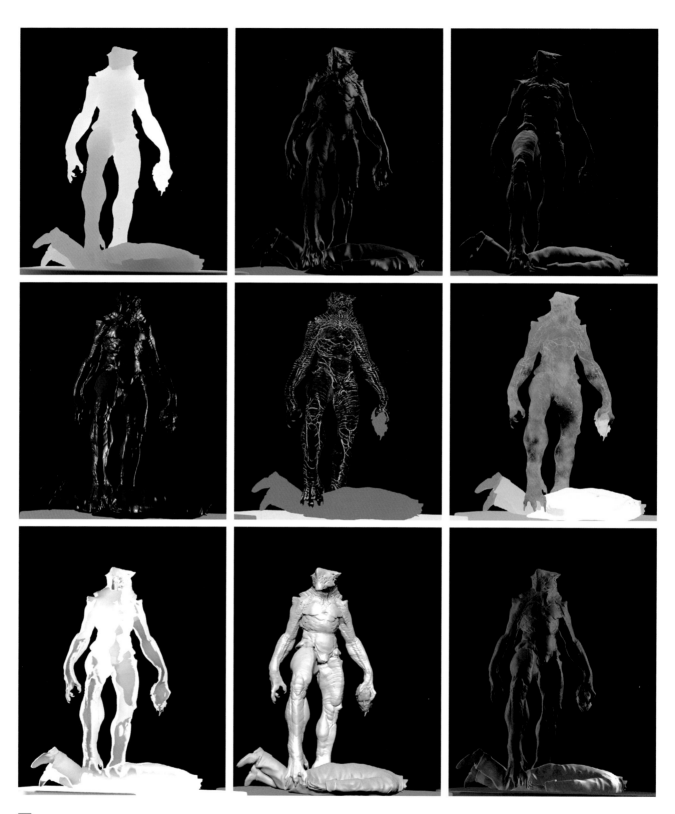

⬆ This page: A series of renders from ZBrush that were then used in Photoshop.

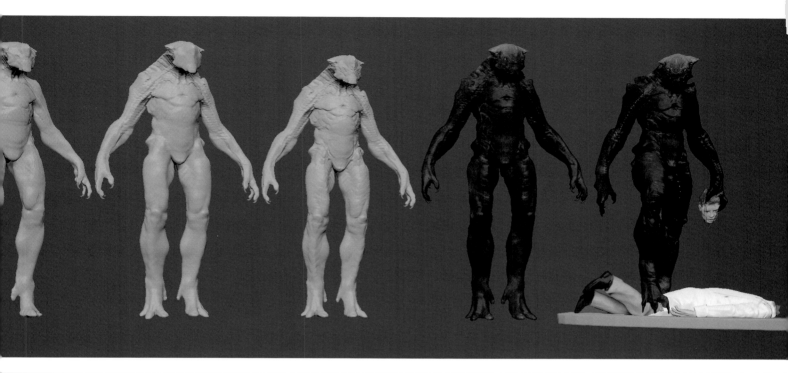

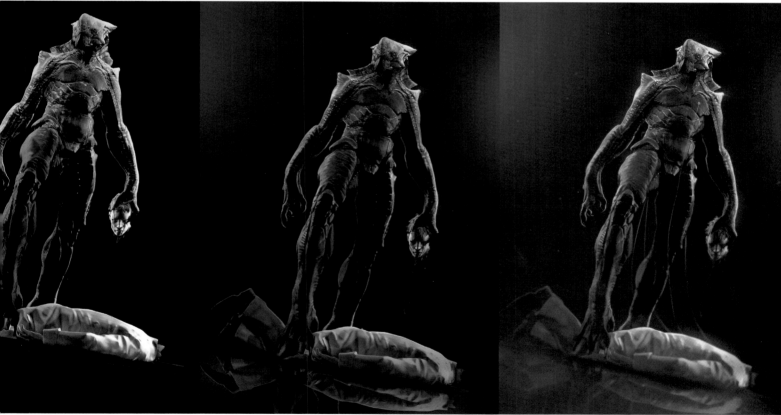

↑ This page: I added in some final touches in Photoshop, and brought up the atmosphere and lighting effects.

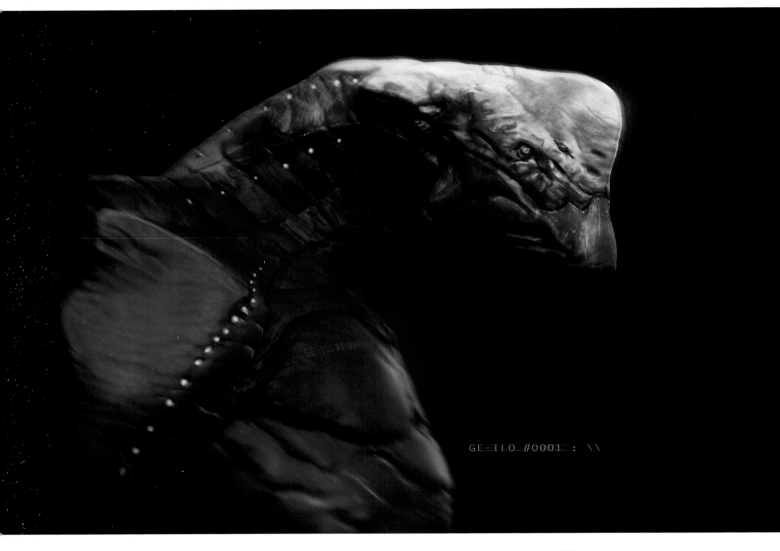

GE-ILO #0001 : \\

⬆ Above: Profile beauty shot of GEILO.
ZBrush and Photoshop combined.

➔ Opposite page: The finished full body of GEILO.
ZBrush and Photoshop.

deep sea creature

ANDREW BAKER

Q: **What was your end goal when you first started working on this creature?**

I wanted to create a large, ominous, floating creature. I noticed a lot of the creatures we were creating for the book were largely land-based creatures, so I thought it would be cool to see something from underwater. As far as the illustration goals, translucency and a degree of bioluminescence were the main things I wanted to achieve. I also wanted to show how large the creature was, so adding the little submarines helped with this.

Q: **What was your inspiration for this creature?**

This was a quick concept that I decided to finish. I was trying to go through some different environments and noticed we hadn't covered the deep sea yet. I've always loved the shots of the various jellyfish that dwell in the deep and their impressive displays of bioluminescence. Of course, they are all tiny, while this guy would be comparable to some whales! I'm always surprised at how little we know about our own planet – and the ocean is one place where there are so many undiscovered things. I like to think of all the different life-forms yet to be discovered, and obviously the bigger the better.

Q: **How does your creature move and search for food?**

I imagined it would be quite a docile creature, just floating along in the ocean attracting schools of fish with its colors. This little trick of light is how it attracts its food. It doesn't prey on anything large really, but feeds mainly on smaller schools of fish and plankton that it scoops up with a set of hanging limbs. These limbs also aid in moving it along. The limbs are equipped with a few fins, but they are definitely not designed for speed. It has multiple mouthparts that allow it to filter the ocean for food.

Q: **Describe the process of creating this creature.**

I spent little time sculpting this guy and mainly wanted to use the external shapes to catch a lot of the light

passes I would create. This gave the creature that translucent look when using the colored shaders as well. A fair bit of painting in Photoshop was done for this piece, on top of the ZBrush renders. I tried to keep the image fairly simple as far as background and foreground, which were really just for providing a context. The main show was all the lights coming from the creature, and most of that was painted up in the final illustration using soft airbrushes and some overlays. It was a fun image to play around with while conceptualizing what to do for the book, and I might continue doing some creatures from the deep after this one!

Q: **During your work on this creature, did you run into any problems or get stuck at any point? If so, what did you do to overcome them?**

I didn't really run into any problems creating this creature. I had a clear image in my mind and went for it. One of the challenges for the piece was always going to be the degree of translucency versus transparency. I found a good solution to this by using soft masking techniques for a color shader from ZBrush, with multiple light passes over the whole model. Once I applied the light passes that I created from ZBrush, I put them on the Lighten and Screen Blending modes and all that was left were the highlights, which gave the sculpt a transparent look. The shaders filled in the rest of the translucent areas, and then it was just a matter of painting.

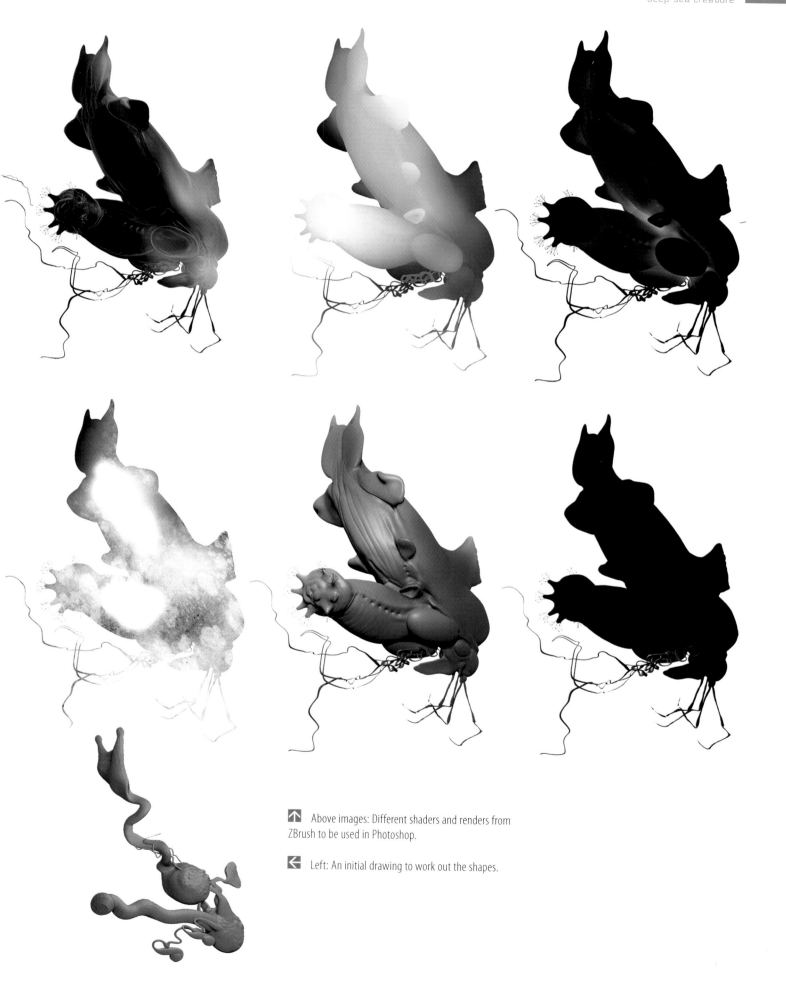

↑ Above images: Different shaders and renders from ZBrush to be used in Photoshop.

← Left: An initial drawing to work out the shapes.

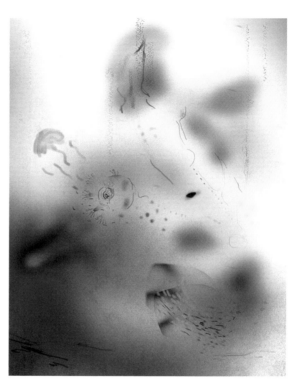

Left images: The Photoshop plates in progress. Here, I worked out some background elements for the final piece and created the overall atmosphere.

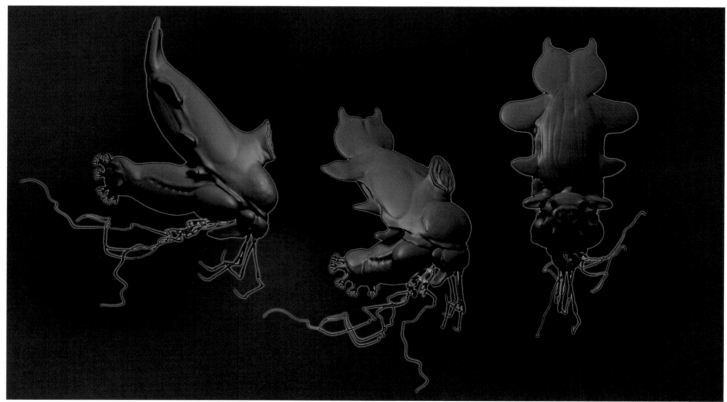

Above: The finished sculpture from ZBrush.

Opposite page: The finished illustration. ZBrush and Photoshop.

flatlands creature

Q: What inspired you in creating this creature?

From the beginning of the planning stages of this book, I had this image in my head. I was watching BBC Africa and I had this idea of some sort of savannah/flatlands in a dry desert-like region where water is scarce. I also have a copy of Wayne Barlowe's *Expedition*, which is one of the most inspiring books I own. I love the detail that has gone into every creature and I would love to undertake a task like that one day. This piece was a small attempt at creating a slice of life from some distant planet.

Q: How does this creature feed and live in its environment?

The first thing I conceived was the idea that they use the sun to make energy, much like plants do. They have evolved these planes on their backs that generate some sort of photosynthesis-like process. The larger creature has a large beetle-like carapace on its back that shades its delicate body from the sun. Their mouths are equipped with a filtering system, allowing them to feed on smaller insects in the mud, which is where they like to wallow until the moisture has all but gone. This makes them a bit of a hassle to other creatures in the area trying to get a drink. They also feed on different plant life in the area, mainly succulents, which, to most of the creatures in this part of the planet, are a good source of water as well. These creatures rely on the sun to survive; the heat is mainly what gets them up and moving.

Q: What other animals did you reference in your thoughts about this creature?

The creatures in the foreground were inspired by tree hoppers and the amazing shapes they come in. I originally had a similar-shaped creature in the foreground, but discussed with the other artists that perhaps a different shape would be more interesting. Upon trying this, I agreed, so I created the three-legged hoppers. I imagined they feed mainly on nectar and have quite complicated mouthparts to deal with the plants, same for the other creatures in the background.

Q: How did you create this piece?

I started out sculpting the giant creature, with a pretty clear idea in my mind of what I wanted him to look like. Normally I would do a series of drawings, but I've found ZBrush has become such an intuitive tool for me to design in now that for a lot of the digital artwork I do – because it's mainly character- or creature-based – I start out there and get straight to it. I did a couple of rough black-and-white studies just to establish some goals for the piece, and I knew there was going to be a lot of work needed due to the fact that there were multiple subjects. I had initially sculpted two creatures, but, after discussing it with the other artists (as I mentioned before), I agreed that a varying shape in the composition was needed. So I sculpted the third creature. Then I thought that something in flight would add to the sense of scale, so I quickly made the flying creatures and started to put them into a basic scene. I found that very little posing was needed, and positioning was key for the composition to work.

Once I had that established and all the elements were working, I did some renders from ZBrush and started compositing in Photoshop. I hadn't originally painted the creatures in the foreground in ZBrush and had to add that in the process. I always enjoy leaving some elements to paint even when I do renders from ZBrush; I find the entire process an organic one that changes piece to piece. Being flexible helps get the best results.

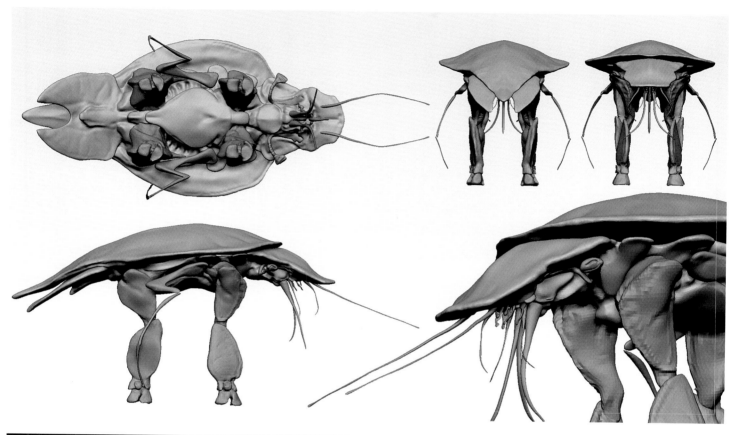

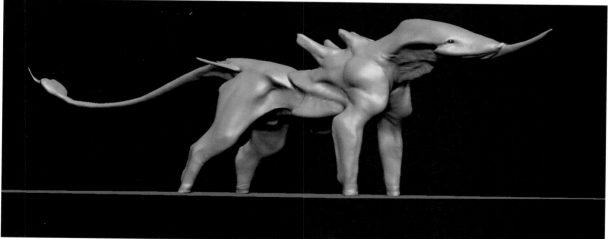

⬆ Top: Finished sculpture of one of the creatures. This was the first creature that led the shape language for the rest of the designs.

⬆ Above: A ZBrush study of an alien creature that never made it to the flatlands.

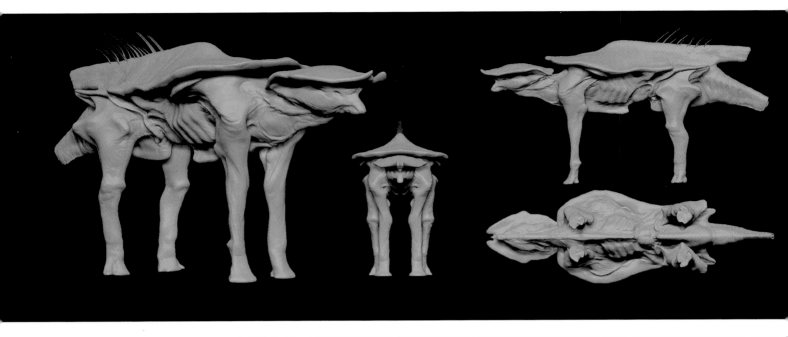

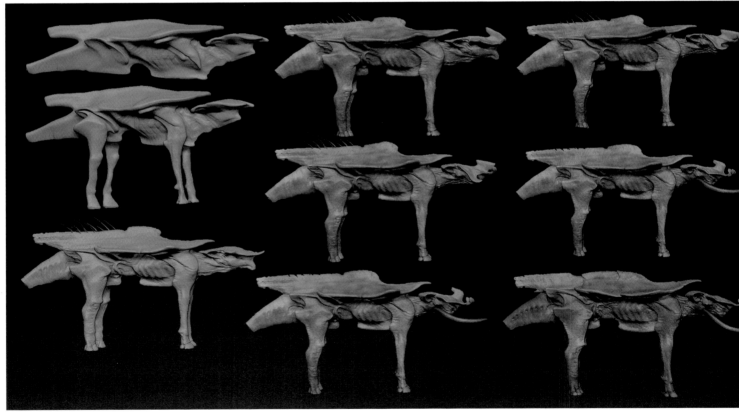

This page: Development of the forms and the iconic shape for the creature. The profile was key for this piece.

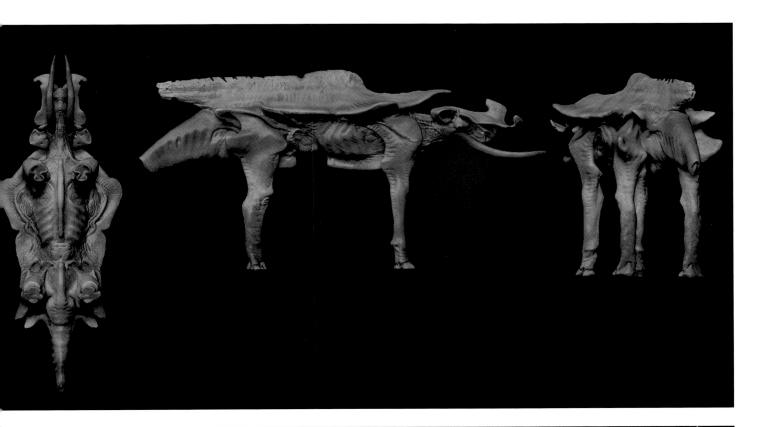

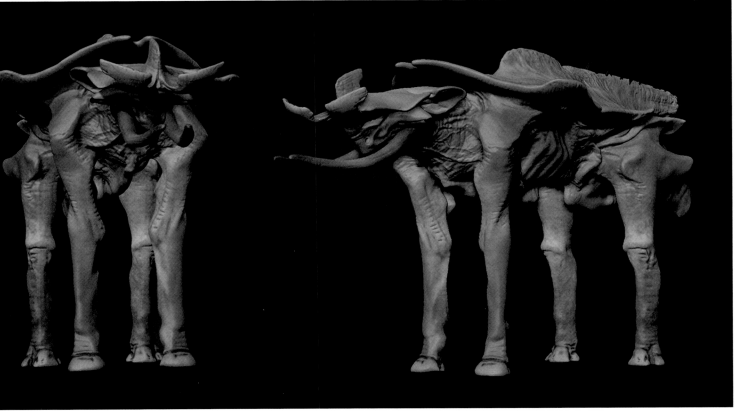

This page: The painted and finished sculpt for the
creature, all done in ZBrush. There was still editing to do.

→ Right: Early black-and-white composition study to determine the placements of assets, and to get an idea if I would need to sculpt more creatures.

↓ Below images: A line up of the cast and scale reference for the piece.

This page: Grey render and two color passes from ZBrush, with a tiny bit of atmosphere painted in the bottom frame.

aris kolokontes

There are two major things that inspire me to create art – the wonders of the animal and plant worlds, and trying to recreate parts of them in my work as a creature designer. I spend a good amount of my time doing research on the web and generally observing the world around me, things that I think will help me in my work. I am also inspired by the work of other artists, from sculptural work to many different forms of art like 2D paintings and drawings, 3D sculpting and music.

I have had an appreciation for creative activities since I was young. My first artistic endeavor was with drawings and play-doh sculptures at elementary school, as all the other children did. I remember liking the feel of plasticine so much that I once ate a piece! Good thing it wasn't toxic! After finishing school in 1999, I contacted the only special make-up effects studio in Greece at the time, Alahouzos Studio FX. They gave me some very useful advice and information regarding molding methods and books and magazines related to SPFX. I went back home and started practising those methods until I mastered them.

I'm self-taught when it comes to sculpting. I learned a lot by reading books like *Men, Makeup and Monsters* and magazines like *FANGORIA* and *Cinefex*, which gave me detailed insights into the FX side of things. I didn't go to a school to learn all of these things; instead I took the trial and error path, which proved to be good for me to develop a problem-solving mindset.

It took me a while to point my finger at what I wanted to do for a living. In 2008, after doing multiple non art-related jobs, I decided to focus on my craft and try to make a living out of it, and I became a concept artist/sculptor specializing in creature design. I started doing as much work as I could and publishing it on the internet for the right people to see. That same year I got my break into the industry when Neill Gorton and Millennium FX in the UK gave me my first job as a sculptor in an FX studio. After that, I worked at Plan 9 FX in Madrid and in 2011 I got to work on my first big budget feature film, *The Hobbit*, at Weta Workshop in New Zealand, where I was based for almost a year.

No matter how much I grow as an artist, I will always look up to the artists who inspired me and influenced me with their work over the years. These are my mentors. My favorites have changed from period to period. During the first years of my career it was the usual suspects, such as Ray Harryhausen, Jim Henson, Dick Smith, Rick Baker, Rob Bottin, Steve Johnson, Stan Winston, Amalgamated Dynamics, Inc. (ADI), Kevin Yagher, KNB EFX, Weta Workshop, and many more. Later, I developed more specific tastes and focused mainly on sculpture. I started connecting with as many talented and successful monster sculptors as I could find through Myspace and Facebook. My favorites were and still are artists like Jordu Schell, Steve Wang, Paul Komoda, Carlos Huante, Miles Teves, Jamie Beswarick, David Meng, Simon Lee, Mark Newman, Shiflett Brothers, Erick Sosa, Takayuki Takeya, Sebastian Lochmann, Aaron Sims, Eddie Yang, Mitch Devane, Mario Torres, Chet Zar, George Steiner, Thomas Kuebler, Joey Orosco, Norman Cabrera and James Kagel. These and many more artists have kept me inspired with their work and continue to make me want to be better with each new creation. I owe a big thank you to all of them. These are just the traditional sculptors; the list goes on with all kinds of other artists…

At the moment I'm working in my workshop in Athens. There are two kinds of typical days for me. One is where I work for me and the other is when I work for a client. When I work for me, it's all fun because I do what I want, how and when I want it. There are no deadlines or art direction so I take my time and enjoy it. I will wake up at around 8 am every day and check my emails while having my morning coffee. Then I go to the workshop to do some work or I do it on my mini workbench in my apartment if possible. Sometimes I have movies playing while I work, and I stop and takes breaks when I feel like it. There are times that I don't feel like working at all, though, and would prefer to spend my day out with friends, especially in the summer! When I work for a client, I will work as much as needed to catch the deadline, but not so fast that I can't deliver my best possible work. So it's a more disciplined way of spending the day. I try to take advantage of all the time I have been given for a project.

Other than my creature design work, I like to experiment with music. I collect my favorite music instruments and enjoy jamming with friends just for fun. Another hobby of mine is to play the photographer/entomologist/biologist out in nature. I go out in search of insects and whatever living creatures I can find and photograph them under rocks, in the forests or near rivers. My photographs are good to use as references in my designing or sculpting process. I also like making movie clips by compiling wildlife-related footage that I have recorded.

My advice for young artists boils down to four criteria I think you must have: a passion for the craft; the willingness to put in long hours of practise; the right networking and marketing of your art; and being a humble and kind character. Then, a little luck will get you there sooner or later.

In the future I will continue to do what I love – experiment with new subjects, materials and scales, and constantly try to expand my creativity as much as possible.

hellhound

Q: **Was this the first creature you worked on for the book?**

Yes, it was. After looking at the Creature Matrix I decided I wanted to do something not so extreme in terms of anatomy. I also wanted to do a predator. Immediately I thought of the real-life predators – lions, bears, all four-legged animals. As I said, I didn't want to do something extreme … I wanted to do something based in reality. I had a mammal in my mind, too. I hadn't decided if I wanted my creature to live in the jungle or desert, so I left that blank at the starting point.

Q: **With this creature, you started with the head. Why did you start there?**

To me, the head is always the most important part … I don't know why … probably because it's where the eyes are. So I try to always start from the head, and then this gives me clues about how the rest of the body will go. For this creature, you can see it took me quite a few different head types before I found the final one – the one with the teeth (see images on pages 74–75). One head looked more like a herbivore than a predator, so at that point I thought I'd save that picture and continue with it another time and make it a herbivore.

Q: **What aspects of that head made you think it was a herbivore rather than a carnivore?**

The lack of teeth. Also, as I look at this image, I see it as a big, heavy herbivore. For me, a predator should look a bit mean and scary. I tried to give that look to my predator. Also, that it is strong, agile, fast – the elements of a successful predator. The jaw is the part that makes him fierce-looking. I also gave him an underbite to be reminiscent of a piranha.

Q: **The profile of the piranha – is that something you thought of afterwards?**

No, I'm just thinking that now. But I could have been thinking that subconsciously as I was sculpting it.

A lot of things go through my mind as I sculpt creatures.

Q: **Looking at the images towards the end, it's looking much more armor-plated. What part of the process were you at when you were experimenting with skin and fur and hair?**

During my whole design process I constantly keep experimenting, adding things, taking things away. For this one, I didn't want to add hair because I don't know how to achieve that in Photoshop. Here is a limitation of my knowledge of the software. In real life I can make hair out of silicone, but digitally I'm limited. So, no hair – so I added armor instead.

Q: **If you were making this one in clay, would you have taken it in a different direction in terms of hair and skin?**

Even when I sculpt in real clay, it's rare that I will sculpt hair because it doesn't look very real. Unless it's a bronze piece of fine art, I wouldn't sculpt hair.

Q: **When you're making decisions about how a creature is looking, do you find yourself pushing something too far and then bringing it back, or do you take it forward in small increments and then decide at some point just to stop?**

Sometimes I have noticed that I've taken something too far or made it too busy, so I go back to earlier stages to refine it. This is an example of that … you'll see in some earlier images that I did a lot of clone stamping of real animal textures on to the model. But it was too busy and not my own work (I had copied and pasted the textures), so I decided to get rid of that as a final image and instead make a nice composition without any clone stamp texture, just coloring and playing with tools in Photoshop. There are so many tools in Photoshop I could use to make this image look a lot more finished, or to add hair or a lot of things, but I don't know how … I'm self-taught and am just learning them. For this book, I learned so much about Photoshop, ZBrush and Sculptris.

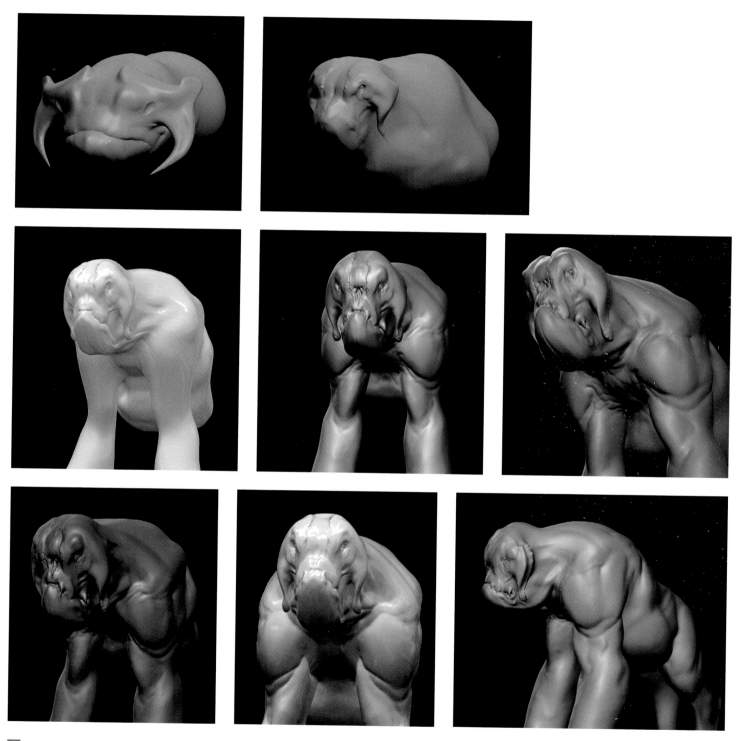

This page: The various stages of development of the Hellhound.

Q: Looking at the recessed nose … Is that a feature you've always wanted to try or did it seem to suit this beast, which is just all mouth and teeth?

I only did one nose for this creature – a nose like a lion's. In some images you can see the skull is like a lion's skull and is very visible under the skin … he doesn't even have lips. I did this to make it scary looking. For the herbivore, I made the nose fat and chubby so it looks more innocent, not so vicious.

Q: This creature looks designed for killing.

Hopefully, yes. That was the goal.

Q: In the end pieces you have him cropped from the shoulder up, but in a few of the ones that are posed he has feet like a lion – is that what you wanted, a running creature?

I thought of lions a lot when I was sculpting this creature. When it came to sculpting the legs, I wanted to give it lion/panther/cat legs. I used a picture of a sphinx cat as a reference. I also have a cat, so I kept looking at his legs and anatomy, too. I guess I could have made the legs a bit more alien, but making them like lion/cat legs was to give him a bit more realism. The head is not like anything we have on Earth, so with the lion/cat-inspired legs, the viewer will make the connection in their mind that it's a believable creature.

➔ This page and opposite page: More progress shots of the model, and some texturing and coloring tests done in Photoshop.

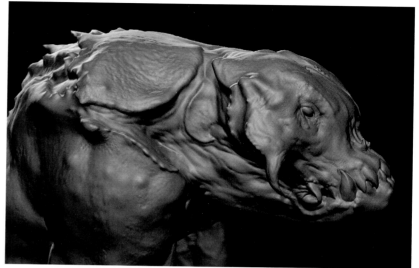

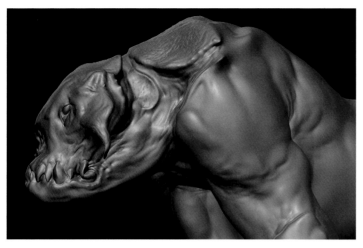

↑→ This page: I decided to get rid of the clone-stamped textures, then I started some composition test images with a jungle background.

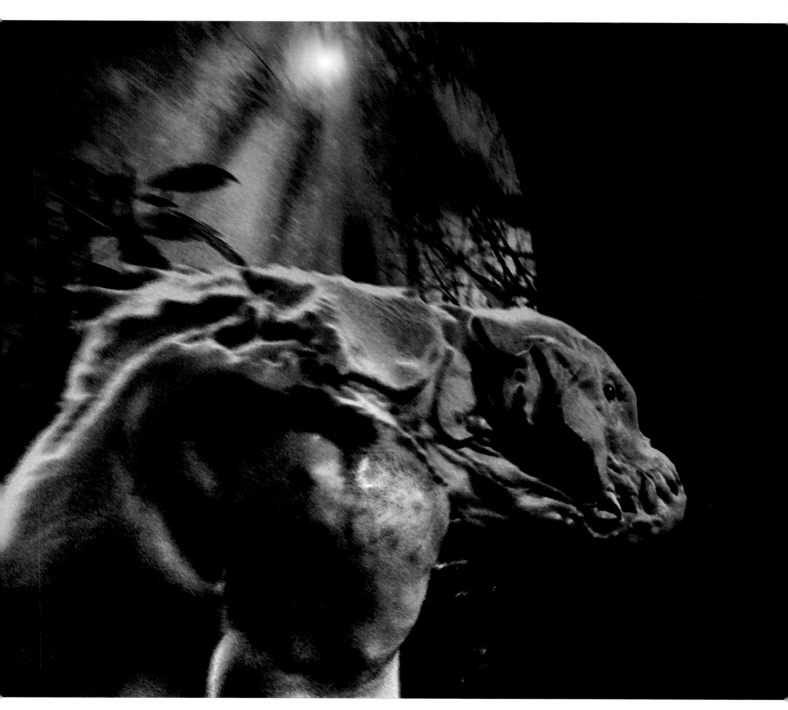

The final image of the Hellhound.
He has just picked up the scent of prey. . .

fungus eater

Q: **What was your end goal when you first started your design for this creature?**

The creatures I had done previously all had four limbs and were very grounded in reality, so for this one I wanted to do something more abstract, anatomy-wise, something not related to a living creature here on Earth. So I thought about how I was going to do that and then started freestyle sculpting. I began with a rectangle of wires (two wires) stuck into wood, and started putting clay around the legs and building the form around it. I kept looking at it thinking it was looking strange, like a turkey or something. It was an early stage. I kept freestyling and adding things, working visually, not thinking so much. At this point I liked how the feet turned out, so I kept them.

Later, it became taller, I raised it … this was after looking at it for a long time and thinking it was looking very flat. After changing the head to the the stalked-eye version, I really got inspired and thought it was going somewhere. This is where the frog-like inspiration came from. I had pictures of a toad I found in a river that had great skin texture, so I used that as a reference to create the texture. From this point on, I had a clear idea of what I wanted it to be … it would be living in a humid environment, it would need to be moist all the time, and it secretes toxins out of its pores, like frogs and toads do. I also wanted it to be very alien-looking.

Q: **You take a lot of great reference photos – can you talk about your process for taking so many great shots?**

Whenever I go somewhere where I know I'm going to be close to nature, I take my camera with me. I like to take close-up pictures of any insect I can find. From a very young age I was excited by bugs, insects, lizards, snakes … I had this thing with living creatures … and now I try to combine it with my work. Whenever I go out into nature, I search for creatures – looking under rocks, taking pictures. I also record the movement of insects and spiders. I can record in high speed, 240 frames per second, and doing this you can see things like a spider running. This is really

helpful for observing and understanding how things move.

So, this process is a combination of things I like to do – I like nature, I like bugs, I like to play the entomologist. I also like to fantasize that one day I could edit all of this and make a movie.

Q: **You want to stay productive, but you can only sculpt for so many hours in a day before you need to go outside and have a break. But when you're outside doing this stuff, collecting bugs and things, doing your hobby, you're still being productive.**

You know us creative people, we want to create all the time. It's not just sculpting for me … other times I want to be creative playing music. It's always something creative … I find it boring to just sit and do nothing.

Q: **Tell us a bit more about this creature. Is this character a male or a female, does it live in a herd, is it a predator or prey?**

I decided it would be a prey creature because it doesn't have a weapon to attack other creatures with. It feeds on fungus, so it's a herbivore. When it is threatened it secretes very strong toxins from its skin pores that make it impossible to eat. Other creatures know it won't taste good. With the paint job I tried to give it colors like poisonous frogs; most poisonous animals have vivid warning colors. Maybe I could have given it more colors …

Q: **The way you created this creature, is it fairly normal for how you work?**

Yes. I begin with very little in mind – that's why I keep changing things so many times along the way because I don't have a sketch to guide me. I end up sketching as I sculpt … and a lot of things might not work to start with but might work later. Some things don't look right and I have to change them.

For my full-body sculpts, most of the time I have some

Above: The body is raised.

Top left: The toad I used as a texturing reference.

Left and top right: The early design process of the sculpt.

plans – how many limbs, etc. Other times it's more specific, like I know I'm going to do an animal that exists or an insectoid-inspired creature or one with two legs. Sometimes I start in ZBrush or Sculptris to give me the freedom to really experiment … I can use the Drag tool and Ctrl Z – all these things you can't do in real clay. I can do all the radical experiments I want, and sometimes they work and I end up with something original; sometimes I have lots of accidents. I work very much with accidents.

Q: What process did you use for deciding which ones of your concepts to take forward? It sounds like your process involves getting to a point where something is bothering your eyes … How do you get to the point where it clicks and you realize it's something you want to move forward with?

I make that decision as I work with a piece. For this one, it was the point where I changed the head. Up until then it wasn't working for me. Then I had the idea that it would eat fungus and I decided to keep going.

Q: Looking at the picture of the toad and the close-up of the head of your creature … around the shoulder area you've added some great texture that you've mimicked really well from the toad. What was your process for doing that?

Again, working layers. First I did little lines, with a little scratching tool I use … the same texture you see on the joint of the elbow. Then I poked little holes with a needle to create bumps (see this technique on page 106). I used different sized needles to get different sized bumps. Then I mixed the clay with lighter fluid to create a slurry of Monster clay, and I applied the slurry in the opposite direction to the holes, filling the holes. ('Monster clay' is a brand of oil-based clay I use.) Then I typically go over it all lightly with a torch to blend it even more, and then leave it for a day or two.

This page: The replacement of the old head with a stalked-eyed version was key to the overall look of this creature. I then added textures and called it done (sculpting wise).

← ↓ This page: Some composition and coloring tests done in Photoshop.

Left and top left: More composition and coloring tests. I decided to use a photograph of a kind of fungus I took instead of the jungle picture I used earlier.

The Fungus Eater final image. The creatures are not
eating here, they are alarmed by a sound.

tree climber

Q: What was the final result you wanted with this creature?

I knew I wanted something that lives in and climbs trees. I had a few animals in mind that inspired my ideas – lemurs, and the ones with the huge eyes that hunt around in the branches … I can't remember their name. But this creature turned out to be a little bit more human. I did know it was going to be a mammal. So from this, I started building the armatures and then added clay. I didn't use any references … I don't like to be restrained, I like to come up with my own shapes and try different things. I wanted to keep this one simple and plausible as well, grounded in reality so the viewer can relate to it. My plan for this one was something that you might see in a jungle, like a new species. It doesn't have anything spectacular or extreme about it when you first look at it.

Q: Did you use the Creature Matrix at all?

I started with the matrix, as I did many times, and then in the process I changed my mind and made radical changes at unexpected times. When something's not right to my eye or if I look too long at a sculpture, I often feel like some things need to change. So then I try to look at my sculpt with fresh eyes to better see the things that need to change, which I do, hopefully for the best. Sometimes I have people saying to me that they like the previous face I had, for example, so I change it. This is all part of my creative process. I've learned that it's never bad to change things, especially if you take pictures of your steps along the way. I take a lot of pictures of my sculpts, using the best angles … sometimes my pictures are better than my sculpts.

Q: How do you imagine this character moves and sounds?

It moves like an ape – it's very agile and fast and has hooks, like a sloth, on its arm … two big hooks that it uses to grab the trees. I go a lot by just the visuals when I'm sculpting. This is the first time I've put detailed back stories to my

creatures and come up with names for them. I found this very interesting because I like to play the biologist when I go out in the wild and take pictures of insects close-up and study them and their habits. The work I've done for this book is one of the best experiences I've had, one of the most creative ones – I got to do exactly what I wanted. During the work for this book, it was first time I tried to combine a sculpture with Photoshop and put it on a background. Sometimes I took my sculpts out into the wild and took pictures there. It's a shame I didn't do the same with the Tree Climber, but time didn't allow for it.

Q: So you started with an armature, no references, you just were blocking something out … Is this process how you would normally work?

Yes, but there are several ways I start to work. I may start a sculpture like I did recently, inspired by the trailer of the movie *Pacific Rim*. My subconscious keeps a lot of this information. But I prefer to keep these images in my mind rather than have them next to me … if I had something next to me to look at, my creature would turn out too much like the one in the movie.

The other way I work is that I have a thought that, for example, I want to make something insect-based, so I'll start thinking about insect shapes and insects that I've seen close-up. I have a small insect case in my workshop and I also have books with thousands of pictures of insects … I spend a lot of time daily just looking at these to get them into my brain. When I want to sculpt a real animal, I start from a picture and then block out the basics. In this case, I wanted to get the exact expression of him, his smile, so I had the reference picture next to me.

Q: Did you do any pencil sketches or did you start in clay straight away?

No, unfortunately I cannot draw. I started drawing at an early age and I was good at it for my age, but as soon as I found out about sculpting I completely forgot about drawing. But I want to learn about drawing again … I see

Left: The wire armature posed and mounted on a piece of wood.

Below: The first stage of sculpting, when I started covering the armature with clay.

all the great sketches others have done in this book. The only way I can sketch is putting it in Sculptris, or sometimes I can do a full-body figure.

Q: **Looking through your progress images, you have four to six different heads … Can you talk a bit about them?**

The last one I changed in Photoshop … I made the eyes bigger. I was looking at a close-up of the one I had saved previously and the face was grainy and had not too much expression … it was kind of grumpy and not looking at the camera, so I thought I'd try to crop a head from a different angle in Photoshop. I now like the expression on the face, almost as if he is surprised to see the camera or something.

Q: **At any point did you get stuck designing this creature … where you weren't sure how to move forward with it?**

I get stuck a lot of times when I need to do something that will take me a lot of time. So I make sacrifices. For instance, for this one, the arm that is behind the tree log, I didn't know how to make that grab the branch so I ended up discarding it and dropping it out of the picture. If I needed to bring it out, the legs wouldn't sit on the tree like I wanted them to. I did a lot of experimenting with them. I knew this creature was going to be on a tree log so I used pictures of logs; the picture in the final image was taken in New Zealand. This creature sits really well on the tree and the shadow is good. That was my major thing … I didn't want it to look like something cropped and put in front of a picture. As this was my first time doing something like this, I can say I'm happy with the result. It doesn't look too much like it is cropped, the lighting is coming from above, it's soft lighting, like the lighting in the jungle.

Q: **In some of the WIP images, on the base near the foot, there is a little sketch of a head that looks almost like a little fish or a lizard … Was that for this creature or something else?**

I just had a piece of clay in front of me and I kept doing different heads that I could possibly add to this character. There is another one with an even smaller head. I ended up never putting them on there; I kept the one I had originally. At this size it's great, I just rub a little bit of clay and if it's warm

I can manipulate it and the clay shows me things and I follow them and squeeze it in different shapes. That's the way I come up with some of my original designs – I grab a piece of clay as big as my hand and I look at it from different angles under different lighting to see interesting shadows … I work a lot like that. I might see a plastic bag that is creating a face … I see faces all over the place!

⬇➡ Below and opposite page: Here, I was blocking in the anatomy and experimenting with some some early head shapes.

↑ Above: An early color test done in Photoshop. Here, the creature has a more demonic-looking head, but I changed it quickly.

← Left: This head was based on a chameleon. I liked it, at first.

→ Opposite page: Close-up of the upper body, side and back view of the sculpt, and a new head version with ears.

Top row: I decided to start digitally coloring and manipulating the sculpt in Photoshop.

Bottom row: Some composition tests, and the replaced head image.

The final image. The Tree Climber has just noticed someone is taking a picture of him and he doesn't seem to be happy about it.

ambush shrimp snake

ARIS KOLOKONTES

Q: With the name for this creature, the Ambush Shrimp Snake, it sounds like you knew what you wanted to make when you named it …

The name was actually the last thing I came up with for this creature. The creature is a combination of a shrimp/crustacean and a snake – 'snake' because of its long body and 'ambush' because of the way it catches its prey. It started as just a piece of wire. The third picture (opposite page, bottom left), where you can see I have added almost like flower petals on the sides, this was the point where I decided to make it a camouflage-based creature that hunts with an ambush technique. I thought it could resemble a flower with vivid colors, and small prey would go to it to smell or eat the flower and then the creature would close its jaws and eat the prey. It's a simple design but it works in nature, so I chose it for this creature.

Again, it's playing with shapes and forms to make it more interesting. It looks like a flower but has elements of a snake, a crustacean, maybe even a cockroach if you look at its back. I used my case of dried-up insects to get inspiration for forms and lines.

The problem with this one is that I didn't know how to photograph it against a background. I had the thought of it coming out of the water but I didn't try it due to the lack of time. So I left it aside for a while, came back to it, and then added more details on the body, more forms, and then I took pictures to do some more experimentation, some adjustments in Photoshop, to see if I was on the right track.

Q: Looking at the images on page 95, it seems you used beads or something for the eyes… Does doing this give you some sense of the creature?

Yes. I put the eyes in during the very early stages. I started from the face, and when I start the face I start with the eyes. The eyes are the most important part of the face. I experiment and play with the position and the number of eyes and of course the size of them. For this one, I started with small metallic ones, then I went to bigger ones, which I didn't like, so I went back to the smaller ones. I went back

and forth until I found what I liked best. Sometimes I sculpt the eyes out of clay, but clay eyes are not round, they are more like praying mantis eyes with a triangle shape. I keep collecting all kinds of little spheres and balls to have a variation of sizes and shapes for eyes.

Q: Scanning across the WIP images, it seems as though the creature you ended up with was much more armor-plated, like a crustacean, than a flower. How did this develop?

The final image is a side view so you cannot see the flower petals, but you can see the armor and the crab-like legs it uses to hold its prey. So here it resembles a crustacean/insect more than a flower. I didn't include the word 'flower' in the creature's name because at the end I chose my final image to be a side view and not full body … in this image you don't even see the snake really. I had problems with how to ground it, how to make it work as a full-body creature, so my final image is a cropped image, because I couldn't pose it as I wanted to. These are the sacrifices I have had to do to make an image work. If the end goal with a creature was to produce a sculpture as a 3D object, I would work on it differently. But since it's going to be published as a 2D picture, that was the best I could do to make the it work. Looking at it now, it looks like it has translucency to it, even though it's just clay with digital paint. I'm happy with how it looks – as a believable creature. But it would be better if I had a more finished piece, with a background.

Q: This creature has had a really interesting development … right the way through there are some strong changes in direction…

Yes, you can see I changed the face a lot … I left one face for two days and kept looking at it and then decided to try something else. Hopefully the last one works, with the close-up face. I used the Liquify tool to make things sharper. I like it because it looks almost like a macro-photograph of an insect, and the coloring and the green background look good. This close-up I'm happy with – it looks real. (See image bottom right on the opposite page).

 Left images: The very first shapes taking form on a piece of wire.

 Rest of page: Further development of the creature. I was designing as I sculpted. The angle and shapes of the back and head reminded me of shrimps, hence the name Ambush Shrimp Snake.

Q: When you change a head on something like this, do you cut the head off cleanly?

Sometimes I cut the head off if I'm not sure what I'm doing is right, and then I start sculpting a new head where the old one was. If I'm not happy with it, I can put the old head back on. Other times if I'm not happy I'll just squeeze it into something new. I always have pictures of the steps so I can show others and have their opinions. I like the experimentation process, and hopefully I end up with something cool-looking in the end. Some changes to the eyes for this one were also done in Photoshop … just small adjustments I did with the Liquify tool.

This page: Here you can see there has been some obvious progress on the creature's form. I changed the head shapes and refined areas of the sculpt, like the belly and limbs.

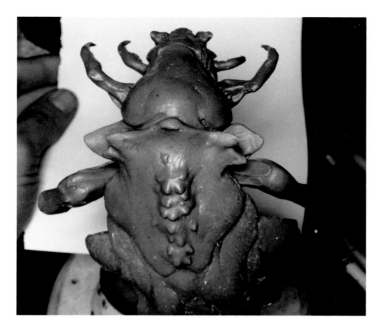

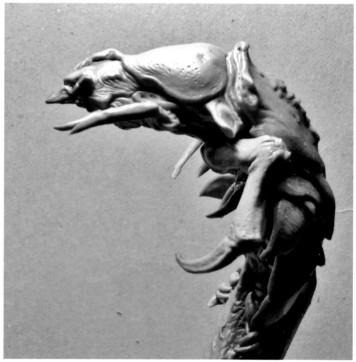

⇦⇧⇧ This page: Another head change and I was finally able to lock down the design. These shots show the finished raw sculpt, and the creature after some coloring and manipulation in Photoshop.

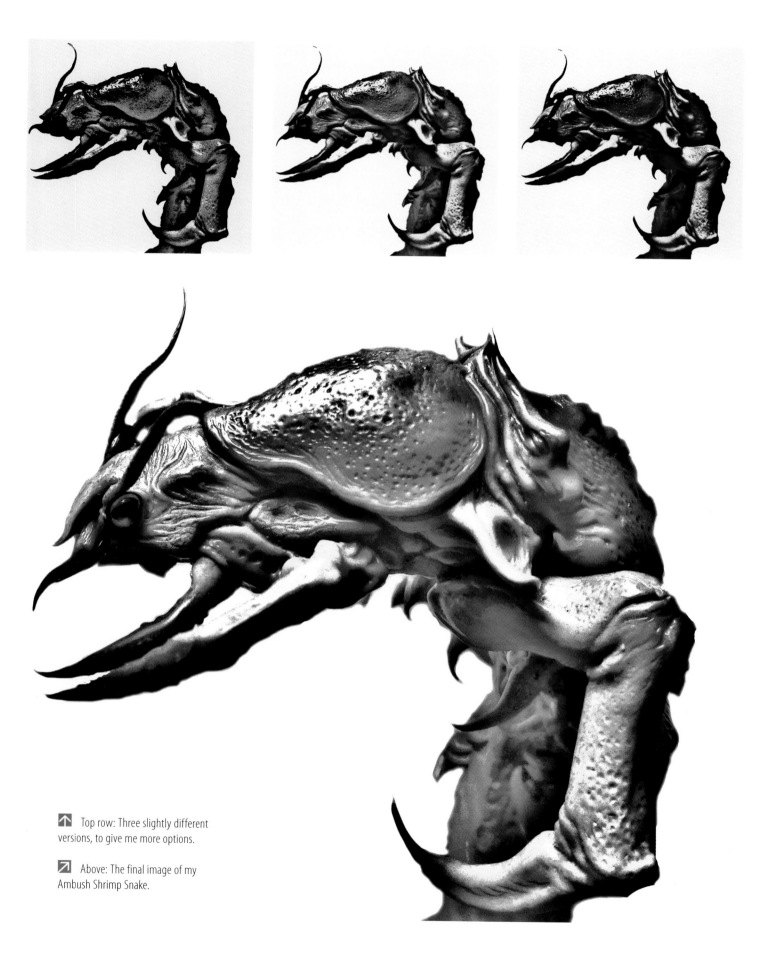

↑ Top row: Three slightly different versions, to give me more options.

↗ Above: The final image of my Ambush Shrimp Snake.

four-legged mantis

Q: What was your end goal when you first started doing this creature?

From the start, I wanted this one to be an insectoid type of creature. Also, I wanted its anatomy to be more extreme and alien-looking than my Tree Climber and my Hellhound … I didn't want it to resemble something you'd see here on Earth. I thought a four-legged insect alien creature would do the job.

Q: What went through your mind when you looked at the Creature Matrix?

The matrix was a great way to give me clues as to what kind of creatures I could sculpt, how could they look, what they could eat, and where they could live. After reading through the matrix, I started visualizing different creatures in their habitats. I wanted this creature to be a predator, and the first insect predator that came to mind was the praying mantis … they are brutal!

Q: Where did your initial inspiration come from?

From observing insects for many hours over many years, but especially inspired by the praying mantis. The front half of this creature resembles a mantis, I think.

Q: When you are faced with a blank page, what goes through your mind? How do you start?

Whenever I start something from scratch, it is always daunting because I have to go through the awkward early stages of development. But from experience, I know that if you get through that first stage and 'fight' your sculpt you will end up with something good. So I keep going and try to work as fast as possible during the early stages (blocking out) so I can move on to the fun part of actually getting in there and sculpting the creature. I want to see results fast! Otherwise I tend to lose interest or end up punching my sculpt into something else.

Q: How do you imagine your creature moves or sounds? Did this influence how you developed it?

When I'm making the wire armature for a creature, I have to decide where the limb joints are going to be and that indicates roughly how the creature would move. In the case of this creature, it moves on four legs and can also make big jumps in almost any direction (to attack other creatures). It is like a locust but with two additional jumping legs. The sound that it would make would be a very high-frequency noise … I can't help but think of crickets.

Q: How many variations did you do, and what directions did you go in to achieve the end result?

This one had almost no variations because I had an idea of what I wanted to see from the start. I had a different pose when I started, but that changed to the final pose after I added the first layer of clay onto the armature. I also added the tail almost halfway through the sculpt to see if the silhouette would improve … it did … it looks more balanced and dynamic with the tail.

Q: If this creature is a predator, how does it stalk its prey?

It stalks its prey with a combination of speed and a lethal poisonous bite. I imagined it would jump on its prey, with great accuracy, and deliver the fatal bite in a split second. Sometimes this creature can be prey for other creatures … it relies on its speed to escape and also on its poison, which it uses as a last attempt to survive if it gets caught.

Q: Did you consider variations – male/female/old/ babies?

I made some group composition images but they didn't quite work for me. At one point I thought about giving the creature some company or a family. All of this is

Continued on page 102…

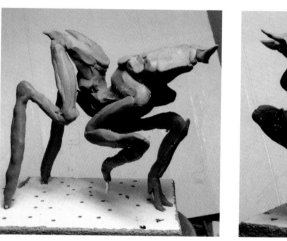

This page: The various stages of development of the Four-legged Mantis. I started with a wire armature and then posed and blocked-in the anatomy. After locking down the design, I started the detailing process.

Left: A group shot of three of my clay creatures.

Below: The Four-legged Mantis in size comparison with the clay Jungle Predator, another creature I developed for the book but which didn't make the final cut.

part of the experimentation process – to try to get the best possible result.

Q: What process did you use for deciding which of your concepts to take forward to a final design?

I always want my work to look good, firstly. Then there are other elements that will make me want to finish a particular piece – like the functionality of the design, its realism, and feedback from other artists.

Q: What did you try in terms of markings – fur/hair/hide/teeth?

I made some curved lines around its body and then complemented them by adding volumes of clay to them to make the creature look more interesting and pleasant to the eye. I didn't think of adding any hair or fur because this is an insect-inspired creature. I didn't think of adding teeth, either … its mouthparts are also insect-inspired.

Q: At any point in the process, did you get stuck? How did you resolve this?

Whenever I get stuck, I go back and look at my sculpt from a distance to see what doesn't work for me. If it's not clear enough, I take a break and go back to it later with fresh eyes. This is the part when I 'fight' the sculpt to make it work.

↑ ↗ → This page: I took some photographs of the sculpt against real backgrounds, and then started adding colors in Photoshop.

↓ → This page: The raw sculpt, and various composition and coloring tests.

The final image.

making goosebumps

MAKING GOOSEBUMPS (below)

This is a great technique for creating realistic-looking goosebumps or lots of different kinds of bumps on skin. Using a pin, I poke holes where I want them; varying the angle of the pin changes the direction of the holes. I make a slurry with Monster clay and white spirit (or gasoline, which evaporates faster). Then I brush the slurry in the opposite direction to fill the holes. I do as many passes as it takes to make the size bumps I want. Then I do a light pass with the torch to smooth everything out, and after it cools down the slurry sets into clay. I can then go over it, adding texture lines, wrinkles, etc. I found out about this technique through an online post. This method is used by make-up artists and artists who make prosthetics.

MAKING MOLDS (opposite page)

1. The finished WED sculpt covered with clear acrylic spray for easier and cleaner release from the silicone mold.
2. I apply the first layer of silicone (100 ml) (RTV silicone rubber for molds). I use a soft brush to apply it and blow air on it with an airbrush to eliminate any air bubbles. I also add a small piece of elastic cloth mesh to the forehead so the silicone won't tear when I take the cast out.
3. I apply a second layer of silicone (100 ml) and another piece of mesh. I color the second layer so I can control the thickness of the silicone.
4. I apply a third and fourth layer (200 ml each) to give the mold more thickness and durability. I use a thixotropic agent to make the silicone paste-like, and then apply it with a spatula.
5. Front half piece of plaster for support (mother mold). I add vaseline to the edge of the front half of the mother mold so that it won't stick with the back half. Then I make and apply the back piece. When dry, I separate the two plaster pieces and start cutting the silicone to remove the clay sculpt from inside.
6. Here you can see how and where the silicone was cut. (The original sculpt was removed here.)
7. Another view of the closed mold.
8. I fill a bucket with 850 ml of translucent polyester resin called MPAL. This is its color before I add white oil color and catalyst to it.
9. I add a white oil color to the resin. The opacity or translucency of the cast depends on the amount of color in the mix. How much color to add depends on the piece's size. I know when it's right by looking at the mix.
10. I mix the color first and then add the catalyst (10-12 g per kg).
11. After the catalyst is well mixed, I hold the mold in position and start pouring very small amounts onto the face area while guiding the resin with the back of a small brush so there aren't any major air bubbles trapped inside, especially around the ears and facial features.
12. I close the mold carefully and start pouring larger amounts while rotating the mold with my other hand. I usually see bubbles coming up to the surface when I'm doing this, which is good.
13. The filled mold waiting to set.
14. I also fill these molds for the bases from the same batch of resin.
15. Here is the resin's color about two hours after casting. It's now ready to come out of the mold.
16. This is the raw cast right out of the mold and shown mounted on its base. First I pull the ears out carefully and the rest comes out with no effort. (I needed both my hands for that so there are no pics.)

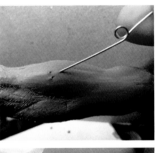
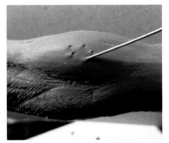

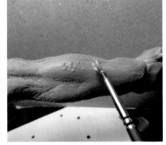
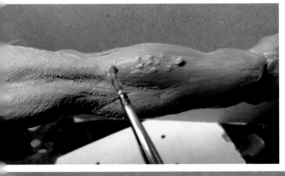

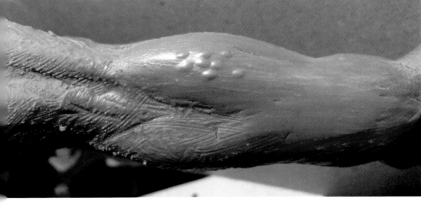

making molds

ian joyner

BIOGRAPHY

When I'm asked what inspires me to create art, sometimes the appropriate word isn't 'inspire' … it's really more of a compulsion for me. I see something that sparks that weird, primitive part of my brain and I just have to create. Despite being lucky that my day job allows me to explore a large portion of that side of my brain, it still occasionally hits me in the dead of night.

Art has been a part of my life, in one way or another, since I can remember. As a very small child, I was in a body cast and spent my days watching sci-fi/adventure films, reading fantastical stories, and sculpting and drawing. My right arm was fully unrestricted while my left arm was free only from the elbow down. As much as I loved to watch and read those stories, what really impassioned my young mind was developing new worlds, creatures and adventures. I even loved augmenting my toys into my own super heroes and monstrous creations using tinfoil and tissue paper.

Once in school, that urge to create got stronger. I spent as much time doodling on the sides of my books and notes as I spent actually doing homework … okay, I spent *more* time sketching than actually doing school work. Luckily, in my home town of Crested Butte, Colorado, my teachers nurtured that drive in me very early, as long as I kept up my grades. They even went so far as to allow me to work on creative extra credit, illustrating key concepts from the stories and events that we were studying.

I'm forever grateful that my creative energy was fueled by my family, friends and teachers from a very young age, allowing me to explore and evolve my interests into more than just a professional career but something that continues to keep me motivated to learn more.

After spending a few years as a graphic designer working on ecommerce websites for flowers and scrapbooking, I joined a friend of mine who had started a company in Florida, creating motion graphics and branding for bands. As we worked together, he allowed me to experiment on different ways to develop such graphics and I began teaching myself a few key 3D programs, such as Maya. It quickly became obvious to both of us that developing characters was what made me the happiest.

Following this realization, my focus turned towards everything 3D. As I watched talented artists on forums like Spiraloid and CGTalk post very free-flow poly-modeling, it felt like 'art' to me instead of just a technical skill. One of these talented artists invited me to test the ZBrush beta, and I was hooked. I became very active in online forums, frequently posting on them, and I entered numerous speed-modeling challenges.

Shortly after, I was contacted by Blur Studio, and, after bonding with the owner over our favorite comics and movies, I moved to California to work on all the properties I had loved growing up. After a handful of years at Blur, I decided to go freelance for a few years.

I have had many mentors at every stage of my life. Some don't even realize they *are* mentors. I would name names but fear I would leave someone out and be haunted by it. I have been very fortunate to have worked with people who are at the top of their field – from artists to studio heads and entrepreneurs. We live in an age when you can learn from mentors online and never even meet them … it's amazing.

I currently work as a Lead Character/Creature Designer at Legacy Effects, formerly Stan Winston Studios. A typical day involves people walking around on stilts or in full mech gear, large vats of dangerous chemicals, and bits of data being pulled into a computer and later output into the real world … not to mention being surrounded by some of the brightest minds in practical effects. In many ways, I'm living like one of the characters I read

about as a kid, running wild in a mad house of super scientists and artistry.

I still like to work on freelance jobs whenever an engaging project comes up, and have also expanded my interests into teaching, which I've discovered has been very rewarding.

In regard to creative pursuits, I've spent the last few years learning to play the guitar and have been hopelessly addicted. I've also decided to go back to my roots in order to reinforce the fundamentals of art – sculpting, drawing and painting traditionally. While I love working on the digital side of the industry, there is nothing quite like working on tangible creations every now and again. It's all so inspiring … every time I see a great film, painting or sculpture, all I can think is, "I want to do that!"

Outside of my professional endeavors, I enjoy spending time with my wife, Hilary, and our animals. Snowboarding, biking, hiking and being outdoors whenever possible definitely awaken my creative spirit. It's also a necessary break from staring at my computer screen at work all day.

The biggest challenges for CG artists are two-fold, in my opinion. The first is a glut of talent in the workforce. Jobs are becoming rarer as rates for entry level positions are decreasing. Without entry level positions, it will become much more difficult to grow into the more demanding roles that the industry calls for. The other challenge is people becoming more enamored with the technology but not paying attention to the artistry. Technology changes so fast, so if you don't have the idea or the skill, you will be left behind by some new automation. Being fluid with the technology but solid with your art is the only way to stay competitive in this new world.

In the future I hope to develop my own IP … I have started refining a few ideas that I hope will bear fruit in the next year or so. It's always fun working with other people to bring their dreams to reality, but I would love to be able to do that for my own concepts as well. I also hope that sometime in my future I will be living in a mountain town with my wife and children, practicing art while teaching younger generations the beauty and fun of creating.

mantapup

IAN JOYNER

Q: What were you looking at in terms of an end goal when you started to design this creature?

I knew that I wanted to do something cute, with more of an adorable presence, since everyone else was focusing on predatory creatures. At the same time, I wanted this critter to have a bit of viciousness, with strange teeth in an open mouth, but I never got around to finishing that.

Q: So, you wanted to do something cute … Did you pull your idea from the Creature Matrix or was this something that you drew up on the fly?

The main takeaway from the Creature Matrix was that I wanted to create an ecosystem so that all of my creatures could exist on the same planet. This creature was originally going to be the one that hunted my Squidsect, but, as I progressed, I decided that these guys were more like bottom-feeders that ingested the scraps as they flopped about on the ground in the mud. The main inspiration for this creature was my dog and cats.

Q: What were some of your main references, aside from your dog and cats?

A big influence on this guy was a picture of a swimming manta ray where you can see its little face, similar to a puppy's face, if you can believe that. Also, my dog has a tendency for trying to jump on my lap to get my attention, and then looks at me with her big, brown eyes. So I wondered what I could come up with if I combined those two references.

Q: Where did the six legs, or four legs and two arms, come from?

Originally I had six legs because, let's be honest, we are making aliens and the easiest way to do that is to add more limbs. As I progressed, I felt it was becoming a little too much like the 'woolah' from *John Carter*, so I added the extra digging limbs and made some other tweaks to help it come into its own.

Q: How do you imagine your creature moving and feeding?

I see him hopping about as he uses the little sensors on his wing tips to alert him to when something falls to the ground, dropped from above by one of the big stargazers and other creatures that might live on this planet. He then picks up these scraps with his little digging arms and uses his shovel-like mouth to separate nutrients from the waste, like a living pooper-scooper.

Q: Did you do any other variations or just the one?

We had a house fire during the middle of the production of this book, and the series of creatures I had begun were lost. This led to me falling a bit behind, so I spent a day sketching out new ideas in ZBrush. After that, I just had to re-top, clean up and Polypaint. There weren't many variations and I didn't feel the need to paint over the model to find its final direction. He came together pretty fast.

Q: Why did you choose the colors you ended up going with?

For whatever reason, this creature's colors just fell into place. A lot of times I like to do color studies to help figure out a solid direction, but this time it didn't feel necessary. As I started to paint him, the blue color palette emerged and I decided to go with it. The end result produced some colors that were a little too vibrant so I knocked them back a bit in the final comp.

Continued on page 112…

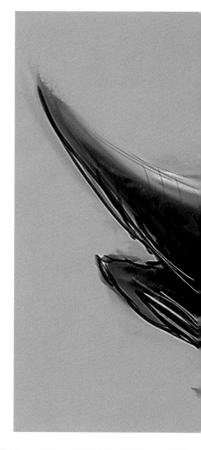

Q: In making this creature what was the most challenging part?

I had a lot of fun making this creature. The most challenging part was to make sure that he had a 'cute' presence and didn't fall into the grotesque. I had thought of adding fluffy fur to enhance his adorableness, but I felt that may be a little too heavy handed. I have always found salamanders to have a very likable feel so I injected an amphibian-like quality into the design while retaining his puppyish characteristics.

➡ Right: My dog and cats – my main inspiration for this creature.

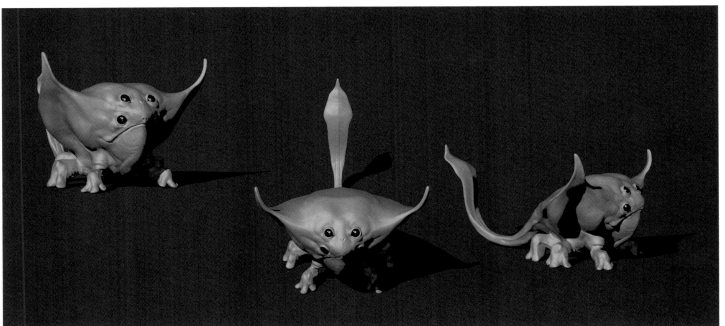

⬆ Above: You can see a study of how the mouth/hunting aspect of the creature would be handled.

⬅⬉ Left and opposite page top: The first drawings of the Mantapup. Often these doodles are done during calls or while waiting for files to save/load.

⬆ Above: The first DynaMesh ZBrush sketch. The Mantapup really came together quickly and took on its own life once I went into 3D.

↑ Top: The final Mantapup sculpt with details and new arms.

↑ Above: The final Polypaint in ZBrush.

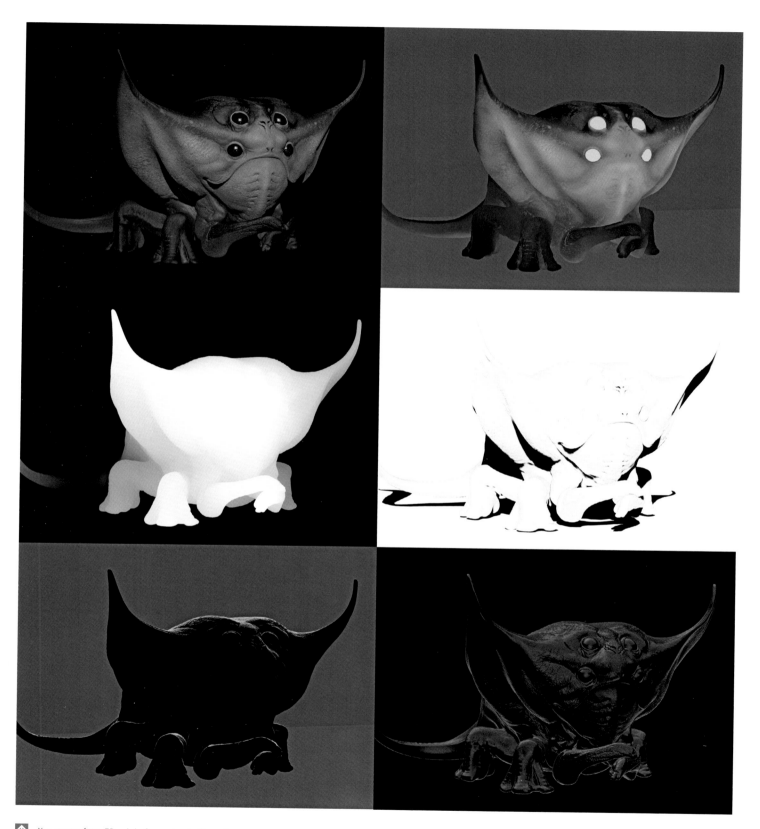

Key passes from ZBrush before going to Photoshop.
A beauty pass, color, ZDepth, shadow, rim and reflection
are often all I like to use.

squidsect

IAN JOYNER

Q: Did you have an end goal for this character?

Going off of the ecosystem concept, and since I had already designed a creature that was low to the ground (the Mantapup), I wanted to create a flyer. I had originally imagined these creatures as parasites, but the sketches have more of a mosquito/vulture vibe with some strange plant-like shapes. I started calling them 'squidsects' as they felt like a hybrid between squids and insects. My main goal was to avoid doing a bug or crustacean since I saw other people going down that path. I focused more on a being that was squishier with less of an exoskeleton.

Q: You have a lot of sketches compared to very few for your Mantapup. So you seemed to go through a lot more variation in the beginning. Can you explain that?

Not until I started sculpting did I have an idea of where I was going with this creature. In my earlier sketches I wanted to find something interesting, and found that I kept drawing vulture-like shapes to which I added tentacles. I thought that would be an interesting look. Once I started working on the silhouettes, I felt comfortable enough with the shapes that I could start sculpting.

Q: For the beginning of your process, what is typical for you … Do you start in sketches or do you go straight into 3D?

As an exercise, I typically sketch a bit for myself, almost as a doodle dump to get some shapes and silhouettes out of my head. Most of the time my ideas come straight out of the sculpture. Once I started sculpting this guy, by about the fourth iteration he was pretty much there. By pulling out his wings and legs, it just came together.

Q: Looking at the progression of your sculpts is interesting. It almost looks like an insect coming out of a cocoon; you can see the shape developing and then it starts to spread its wings and then it gets a little bigger. It's cool to see

you push the forms further and further. Tell us about how this guy sees, senses and eats.

I like the idea that these squidsects do not see exactly as we would expect. Based off creatures in our world, ones that can see a visible spectrum of color including infrared and ultraviolet, I thought it would be interesting if the two orbs in the front of the creature acted as eyes without actually being 'eyes'. Beneath the orbs is a pitcher-plant-like concept of an exposed stomach. The tendrils surrounding it would help pull food into the pot. Next to that, two additional orbs can be seen, which I envisioned as sensory organs. What I find interesting about this creature is that it has recognizable features in an unrecognizable fashion.

Q: Obviously he flies, but is he mostly on the ground or does he mostly fly?

These flyers mostly glide since their wing span is not long enough to propel them through the air. I envisioned that their legs could spring them into the air, at which point they could use their large scoop-like parachute wings to hunt and find mates. The bioluminescence on the wings and body is primarily a mating feature; in later versions I removed it from the wings.

Q: How much time did you spend experimenting on your color variations, and what made you go the route you ended up going?

I didn't really have a vision of what I wanted color-wise, so I did a color study sheet in Photoshop. In these studies, I had very watermelon-based themes and some that were much more in the flesh tones (which I later applied to the Stargazer). The colors that caught my eye were in the blue, purple and green range. Often, I will just begin the color studies within ZBrush, using Polypaint … but when I don't have a clear idea, nothing beats Photoshop for a variety of quick turnarounds.

Continued on page 120…

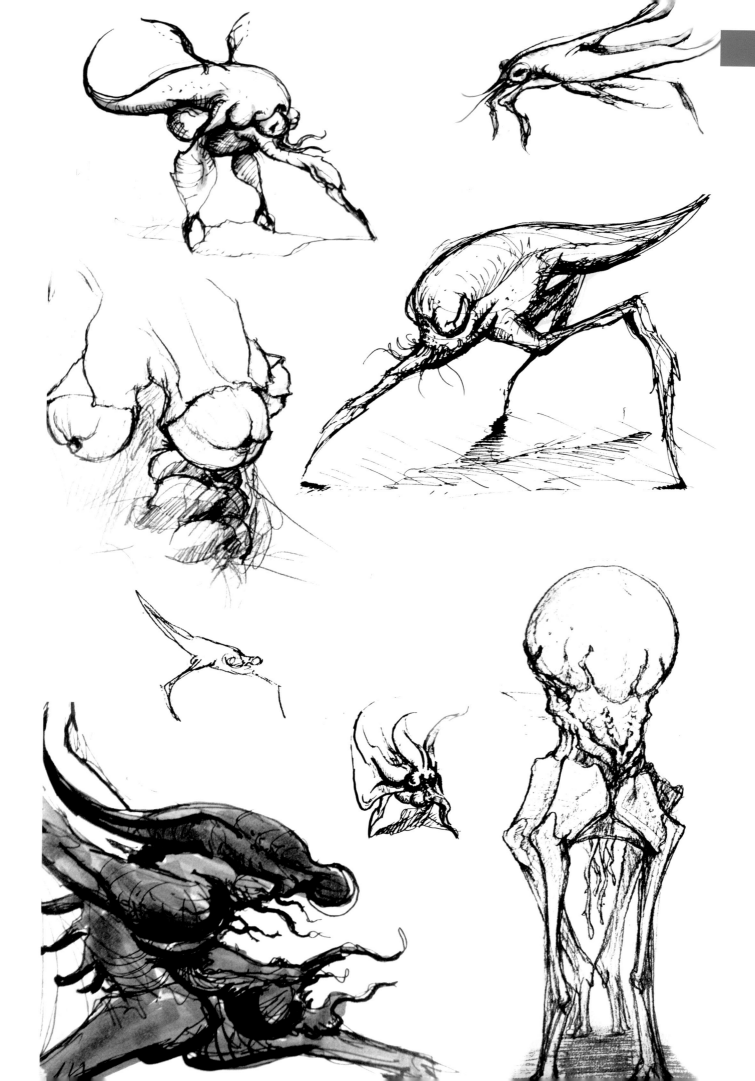

Q: Did you use the Creature Matrix for this at all? Or, if you didn't, what do you consider him to be – omnivore, herbivore?

I definitely see these as a predatory species. I imagine that they use their bioluminescence to not only attract mates but to help them act almost as a flying anglerfish, attracting their prey. However, there is a setback with this method of hunting – the glowing attracts the attention of their own predator, the stargazers…

Q: What was the most challenging part in this process? You have a final image with multiples of the creatures … Did you spend a lot of time working on composition, or colors?

The most challenging part was the composition. After I completed the standing image, I knew I wanted to show them as a flock. I had a few different ideas for how I wanted to handle the bioluminosity as well as the transparency of this creature's wings. In hindsight, I wish I had attached the wings to a more obvious location to show off the transparency … as in the final comp, you really only notice that feature if you know what you are looking for. Of all the creatures that I created for this book, I performed the deepest color exploration on this creature.

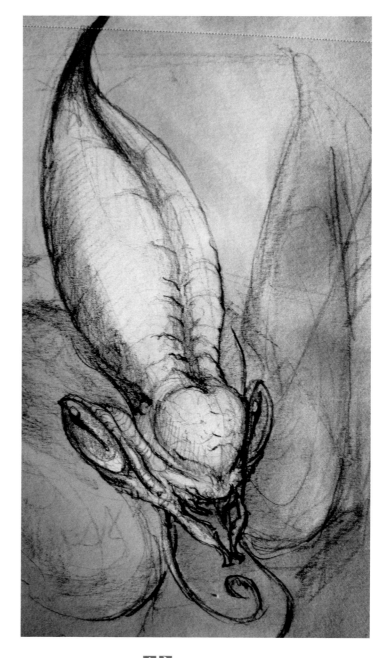

↑ → Above and opposite page: Some studies of the silhouette and 'feel' for the Squidsect. I was still very hung up on bug-like ideas at this stage.

ian joyner
squidsect

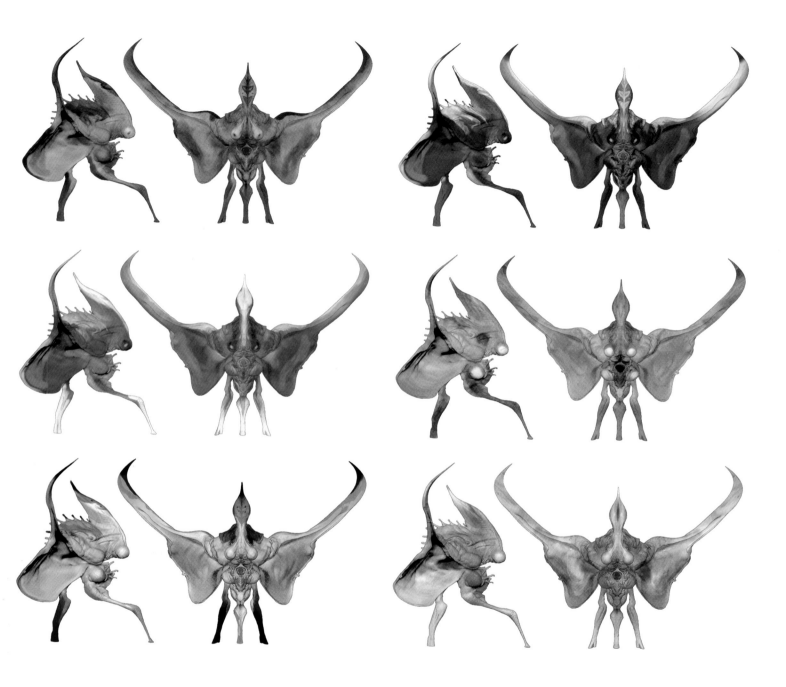

△ Above images: When in need of variation, I like to use Photoshop to come up with a large number of ideas before committing to anything in ZBrush.

◤ Opposite top: From a sphere and using DynaMesh, the Squidsect emerges as a sculpture.

◄ Opposite bottom: Final Squidsect sculpture in ZBrush.

↑→ This page: Different versions of the bioluminescent feature of the Squidsect. The blue/purple option was decided on for the final group shot.

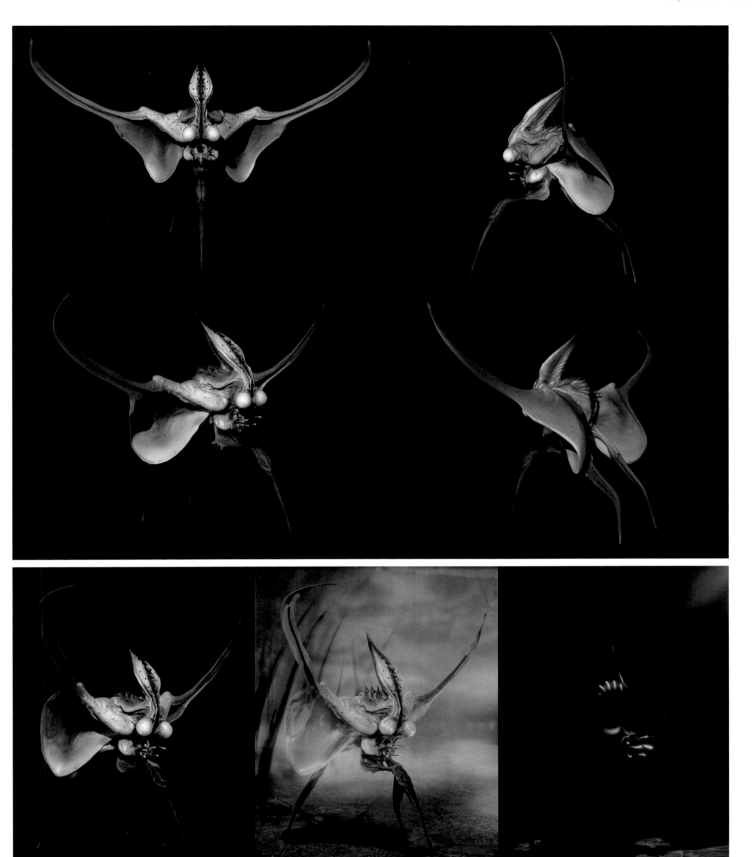

This page: Final Squidsect sculpt and paint job in
ZBrush. The three images immediately above show the
final stages in finishing the 'hero shot' (final lighting/color,
background, atmosphere and details).

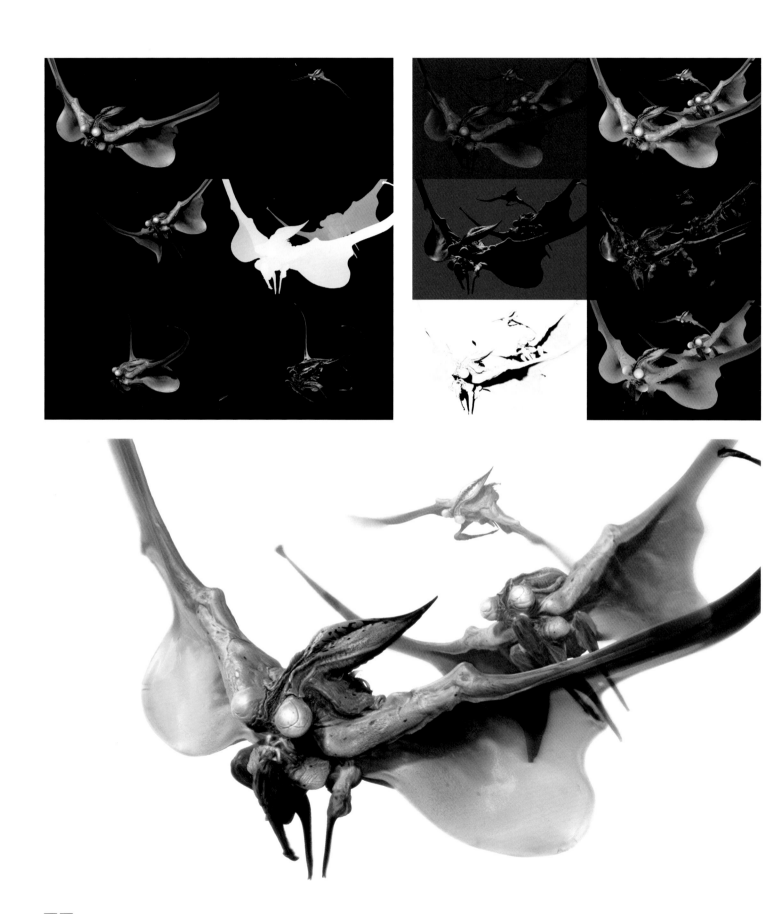

↑ ↗ This page: Various passes of the different flyers, using beauty, color, rim, reflection and shadow.

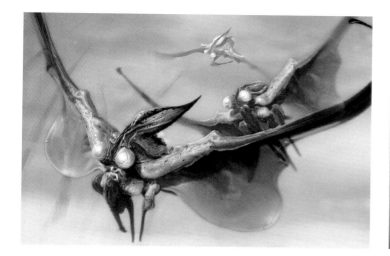

This page: The final passes with atmosphere, lighting, details and blurring, to bring the action to life.

stargazer

Q: You said you wanted to have your creatures all in one ecosystem. In what order did you design your three creatures?

The initial sketches for all three creatures were created in one sitting. In some of the sketches, you can see that the ideas cross-pollinated as I completed the final looks. They all evolved side-by-side and began to work themselves out as three distinct creations. The Mantapup was the first of the three and by far the easiest in terms of development. Once he was completed, I moved on to the Squidsect, which, thanks to many of my doodle dumps, took on a life of its own. The Stargazer was definitely the most difficult part of this discovery process. It was originally envisioned as kind of a goofy, comical character. After finishing the other two creatures, I felt that this ecosystem was lacking a more vicious, predatory species.

With the Squidsect's bioluminescent feature, I realized that these large Stargazer beings, with their strange up-turned eyes, would be a perfect predator for them. Though the Stargazers were originally intended to be herbivores, with a little exploration they worked much better as hunters. Often when developing a creature, you may find it fits into another category better than what you had initially intended.

Q: You have quite a lot of sketches of snail eyes. You have one image where you're just showing a few paint-overs of your sculpt, trying to incorporate those eyes…

The first image in that series is the initial DynaMesh sculpt. I let this sit while I developed the other creatures. When I came back to it, I knew that I wanted to keep the snail-like eyes that could move independently of one another. I wasn't entirely sure at that point how far to push the features … more comical or more creepy. Once I determined the direction, the stalk eyes really seemed to fit well.

Q: Initially this creature was more goofy and a herbivore, and then doing those sketches it looks like you hit something you liked in making him a predator, and almost grotesque…

I began developing this creature with bright colors and very over-the-top features. I used bright reds, pinks, black accents and whites, and developed a very comical face that produced a rather whimsical design. Once I determined that this would be a predatory species, and had already named it 'Stargazer', I realized I needed to go in a different direction. After doing a few quick sketches and a paint-over of the existing model, I settled on the more sinister final design.

Q: How does the creature hunt the squidsects?

I like the idea that, using their cocked-back heads, they would have the ability to shoot out and snap at their prey like a turtle. Standing very still in the breeding grounds of the squidsects, they would wait for unsuspecting victims to get within range and then attack. Very much an ambush predator. Another thought that I was developing is that they would emit a smoky vapor from their mouths that attracts the squidsects.

Q: What was the biggest challenge in creating your final image?

These creatures took on such a different look from every angle that a group shot just made sense. After posing the foreground stargazers, I realized I needed a third to help balance the image. Initially, I tried simply duplicating one of the existing gazers but decided that this might break immersion for the viewer.

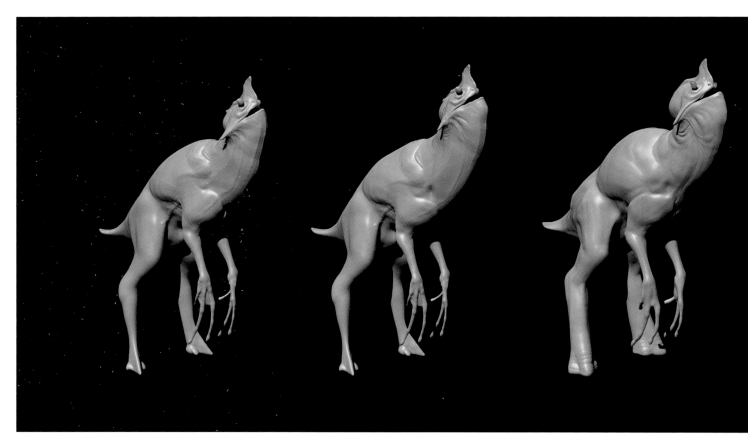

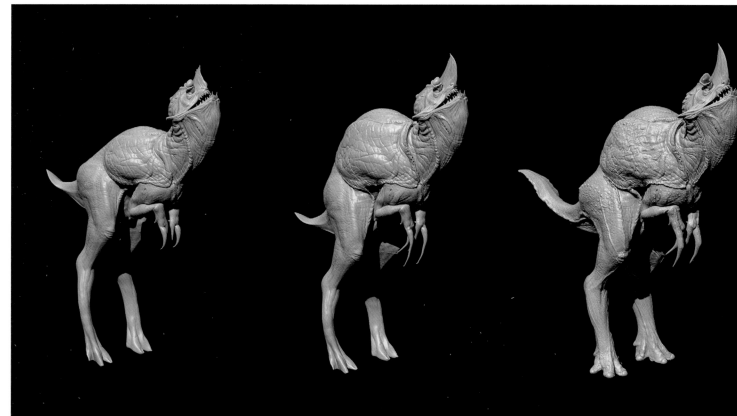

⬆ Above and top row: From a sphere in ZBrush using DynaMesh, the Stargazer came to life. The final stages moved away from this creature's silly aspects and explored its darker side.

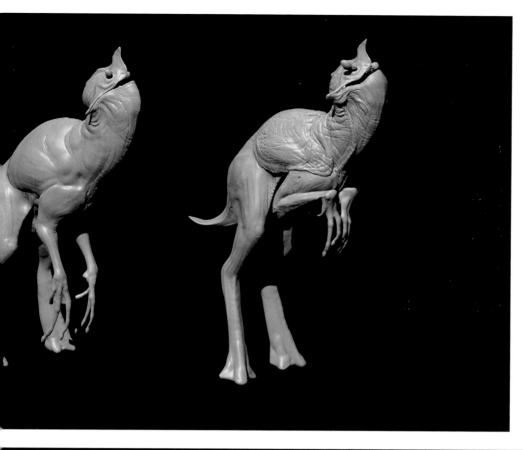

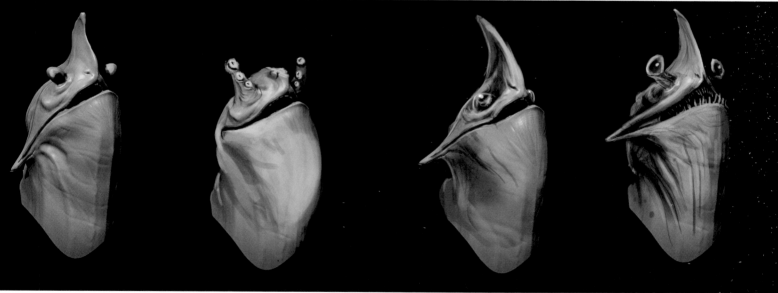

↑ Above: The image on the far left is the initial ZBrush sketch. Once in Photoshop, random ideas were sketched out to determine the final direction.

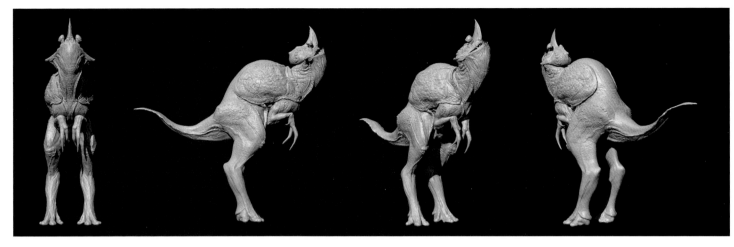

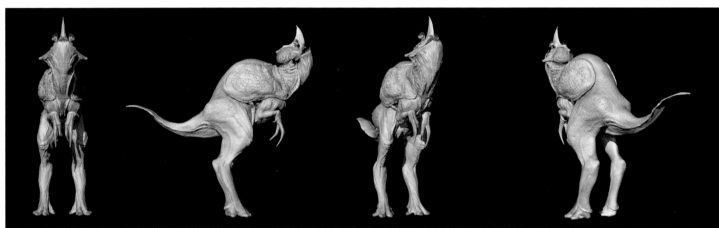

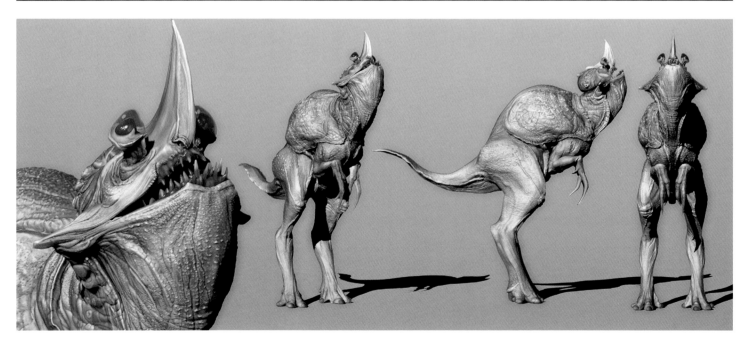

Top: The final detailed model. Middle: The final paint job. Bottom: Work-in-progress shot of the creature with the creepier vibe and a revised paint job.

Above and top images: The final composition was all about atmosphere. Using the threshold in Photoshop, I checked how its values were reading at an extreme.

Left: A close-up of lunch time for the Stargazer.

other concepts

↑ Spacepope

↑ Mountain Eater

↑ Oversized Omnivore

These sketches, speed sculpts and designs are ideas that didn't make it past the early ideation stage, but present exciting would-be creatures and concepts to explore in the future.

↑ Spaceskunk

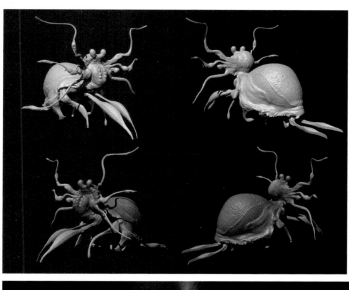
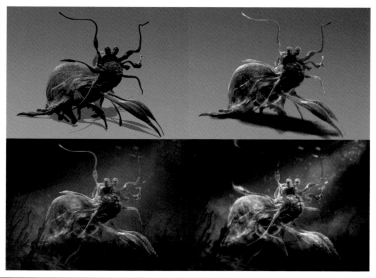

Jellyshrimp

james van den bogart

I find inspiration in anything and everything. Most often I'm trying to find a shape, a color, a form – something I can relate to in some way and translate into a work of art. I'm also inspired by so many artists. I can't begin to name all of them but a few who are perhaps more relevant to this book are Gio Nakpil, Andy Nisbet, Jamie Beswarick, David Meng and Simon Lee, just to name a few. Their understanding of form, shape, color and flow is beyond anything I can comprehend at the moment. Looking up to such great talents constantly inspires me to keep pushing for more from myself.

In high school I doodled a lot in my notebooks, trying to recreate works by Jeff Jones and Frank Frazetta. Following these types of dudes is setting a high bar but it's what I've always felt was necessary to get better. I have always drawn and doodled but it was never a passion for me. I was into sports and was a three-sport athlete in high school, playing football, basketball and track. Sports ate up all of my summers and most of my weekends starting from 5th grade to my senior year of high school. It wasn't until more recently that drawing and art became number one for me.

When I graduated from high school, I attended the University of Minnesota and focused on sports medicine. The first few months of school went great – I was setting curves in math classes and taking care of business. Slowly, though, I started to skip more and more classes and party a lot.

The summer after my freshman year I received an expulsion letter. I talked with my girlfriend at the time (now fiancée) about my expulsion and we decided that I would attend the Art Institutes International Minnesota on a whim, for fun. Here, I had a blast. I didn't know that Photoshop or 3D programs even existed before that. I dove head-first into my three-year degree.

My big break came six months before graduation when I attended SIGGRAPH for the sole purpose of getting a job. At first I was really intimidated by the prospect when I got to the job fair, and I ended up walking out. On my way out I saw my friend and together we went inside. I talked to one company, ArenaNet. I was lucky enough to have my portfolio with me and was able to score a six-month contract on the environment team. Six months later I moved to where my passion lay – the creature team.

Two people who I call mentors are Daniel Dociu and Danny Williams. These two have different philosophies about art, and I have learned so much from both of them. It's easy for me to say that I would not be where I am today without these guys. Daniel was my Art Director at ArenaNet and taught me so much about everything, from aesthetics to lighting and color. Danny helped me a ton with sculpting and the 3D side of things. A lot of our interaction was working alongside one another and spit-firing information back and forth. The wealth of knowledge that these two possess is invaluable and immeasurable. I can't even begin to thank them enough for how they have impacted on my life.

I am currently working for Sony Santa Monica. My typical day consists of office banter and sculpting. Most of our character pipeline is spent in ZBrush, where we can concept, sculpt, paint and decimate our characters to ready them for use.

I'm huge on video games and try to play them as often as possible. I just spent the last year buying old Super Nintendo games that inspired me while I was growing up. I tell my fiancée it's research for my job! Other than that, I love CrossFit, which has been a really nice stress reliever for me over the past two years and it's helped me shed un-needed weight I put on from long days sitting at a computer.

The biggest thing I can say to anyone trying to break into this industry is something no one told me: No amount of advice will help. You must work at this every day and have a passion to do it every day. You have to spend the rest of your life doing this, so make sure it is first and foremost FUN. If you find yourself looking at the clock or complaining all the time, then it's probably not for you. Since I am a huge sports nut, I'll never forget what my idol growing up, Barry Sanders, said … something along the lines of when it's no longer a game or fun, it's time to step back and re-evaluate what it is you want out of whatever it is you are doing. In his case he was talking about his football career. So, in short, my piece of advice would be do it because it's fun and for no other reason.

I can't speak for all of CG but I think the biggest challenge for character artists right now is having to become better at multiple things, specifically design. Since outsourcing is so prevalent these days, companies no longer have a need for people who can just make a concept into 3D. So being good at multiple disciplines will make us invaluable down the road as the industry starts to mature and find its groove.

chub

Q: **What was your end goal when you started this creature?**

The idea behind this creature was to see if I could make something interesting out of a circle. I drew a circle on a piece of paper and tried to find a way I could pack a cute creature into it. Then I moved into the tadpole creature – with its chubby cheeks, softer body, a little smirk and smaller eyes, so he looks like he's squinting and kind of smiling.

Q: **Did you use the Creature Matrix for this or was it a bit more free-form?**

This was a bit more free-form. It slowly evolved from a bunch of different things so it isn't really a good representation of the Creature Matrix.

Q: **You talked about a sphere for your inspiration, and then tadpoles. Were there any other things that inspired this creature?**

A gorilla, with long arms and stubby legs. Then penguins. I then rendered out the scales and tried to find the frequency. Then it started to look like a kung-fu panda rip off, and that wasn't the best route for me or catering to my style.

Q: **The scales are really nicely done – did you sculpt them by hand?**

Yes, I sculpted them by hand. I used a technique where I drew a chequer board on them and then pushed and pulled and masked them off to get a layered effect. Then I went it on each one and started sculpting and reinforcing the edges so they felt solid and layered, and more natural.

Q: **How do you imagine this character moves and sounds?**

It moves like a mini gorilla, it's kind of a big ball of meat – it hobbles around and when it starts running it is on its hands more than its feet, so the feet don't serve a purpose apart from enabling it to sit down and prop itself up. I imagine it having high shrieks and shrills.

In one of my WIP images, I worked through different heads – that's when it started looking like the kung-fu panda and getting away from my tastes. I tried a squared-off owl head, then a more lizard-looking head. At this point I decided to get rid of the scales after some feedback from some of the guys on the blog. (This shows how beneficial the blog was for all us … you'd post an image one night and in the morning have comments and be able to push the image even further.)

After I got rid of the scales, I started to create a demon-looking head (I tend to make things look angry and mean, so this fit me better). Then I tried to add more planarity to the shoulders – you can see that on the ridges – trying to make him look more imposing. I started to think about German WWII helmets, with their armored skulls, and started to build it from there, reinforcing some of the lines, which catered towards texturing it, darkening it or lightening it.

Q: **It looks like you did a lot of exploration for this character – explored lots of different shapes and heads and also did a lot of exploration color-wise. What were your thought processes behind all this?**

I didn't want to just do what I normally do. If you look at the colored versions you can see a red one with tan – that was sort of the logical progression, but then I wanted to challenge myself to take things to the next level. I tried a few things and if something worked and had potential, I wanted to take that to the next step instead of just doing things over and over. So I ended up not going with the red one. A few people on the blog supported the yellowish-blue one with the orange, so I went with that for the final. I think that was the right decision in the end.

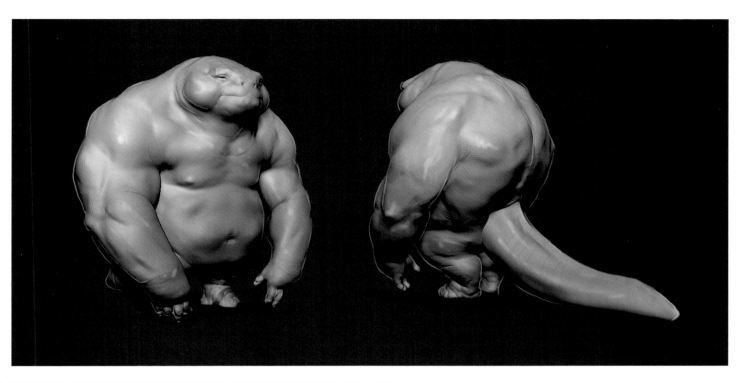

Above: First block in for this creature. He was meant to be much cuter and more amphibious at the beginning.

Left and bottom: Evolution of the character where I attempted to use pangolin scales to add more variety to him.

Q: In your final image your character has fire and smoke in his mouth and he's chasing some little bees. Can you explain that story element to the character?

I pictured him being in the pine barrens, in abandoned places that had been decimated by fires where new life was just starting to sprout. Nothing can really hide in those areas, so everything is exposed. When he chases bees he can smoke them out of their hive.

Q: What was the most challenging part in this design process?

Adding the scales. I fell more in love with the scales than I fell in love with making it a better creature. At that point I was losing it a bit and I almost gave up. So I started to explore heads to try to make the creature better. It's one of those things you innately do to improve your workflow.

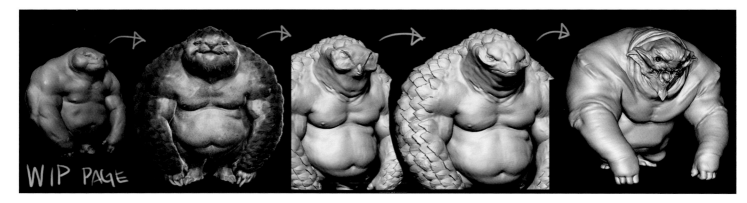

WIP PAGE

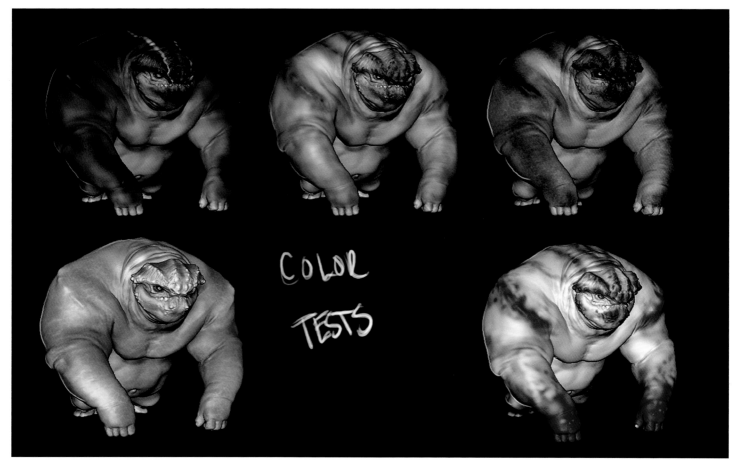

COLOR TESTS

⬆ Top: Work-in-progress images.

⬆ Above: Color test I frequently do to try something I wouldn't normally think to use.

↗ Opposite top images: Render passes used to composite the final image in Photoshop.

➡ Opposite bottom: Prelim for my final render. It became too noisy and needed more clarification between all the elements.

helix camelus

Q: What was your end goal in creating this creature?

To have fun with one of my creatures. Sometimes you can take things too seriously, so I wanted to keep it fresh and have people look at it and think, "That's a fun guy".

Q: Did you use the Creature Matrix or what was your source of inspiration?

Since I wanted to have fun with this, I thought of kids blowing bubbles and wanted to mimic that. He has this mucous on his slug body that he wraps up into the structure on the top of his body, and that then secretes the mucous. When he runs, the bubble expands out of the back.

Q: Does the bubble serve a purpose?

The bubble's purpose is protection. These creatures live out on the prairies and in shallow forests so they are exposed and their only way to get away from predators is to run. When the chasing predator runs into the bubble, it pops and bursts in its eyes and has a stench to it, and this gives the creature a bit more time to get away.

Q: Did you do many sketches or variations to prepare for this character?

I was just sketching randomly in my sketchbook, scribbling on the page at first, laying some little nicks on the page to try to see something – then I saw this thing emerge from the scribbles, saw its basic structure, and I wanted to emphasize some more structure. He's a slug so he's a little shapeless in the middle, but I wanted him to have a hard surface that can slime up.

Q: Is that process normal for your development cycle or did you try something new?

Most creatures I start by opening my sketchbook and scribbling and drawing random things. Very seldomly do I draw a specific creature with a purpose. A lot of times I'll take a blue lead pencil and scribble around and draw circles and see if I can see a face or a body, then I'll add some limbs. If I do see something I'll go over the top of it with a felt-tip marker to emphasize and lock the idea down.

Q: This character is prey and uses the bubble as a defense mechanism. What does it eat?

This character runs through fields of daisies, so I imagine it would run up on butterflies and bees, general insects flying around, and the bubble encompasses them and knocks them down and then decomposes them.

Q: Does it have teeth?

He's got these glowing orange appendages in what I think is the mouth area … it can't really reach anything with its long legs, so it has to squat down to eat things. All of its reproductive and eating organs are at the bottom.

Q: At any point in this process did you find yourself having to solve a problem or was it a pretty straightforward design?

This was a rare case when I had a very clear idea of what I wanted, so the execution was pretty quick. I just had that one sketch in the sketchbook and the sculpt took about 45 minutes, and then I did some quick paint-ons and final renders.

→ Opposite page: Here you can see my initial block in process using DynaMesh. I made two separate shapes for top and bottom.

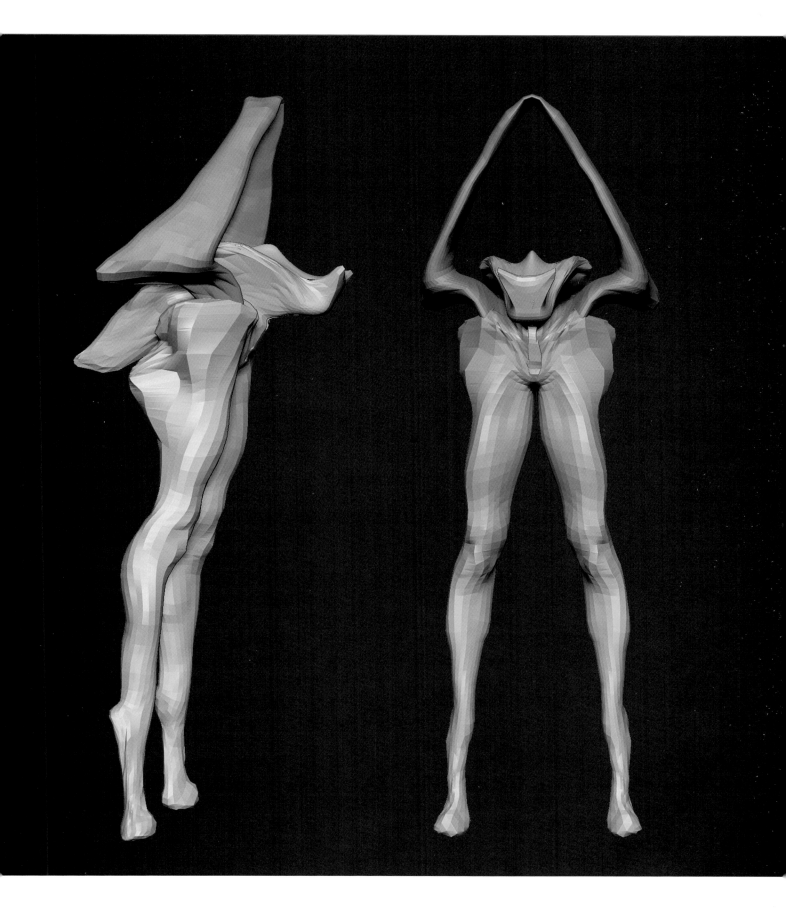

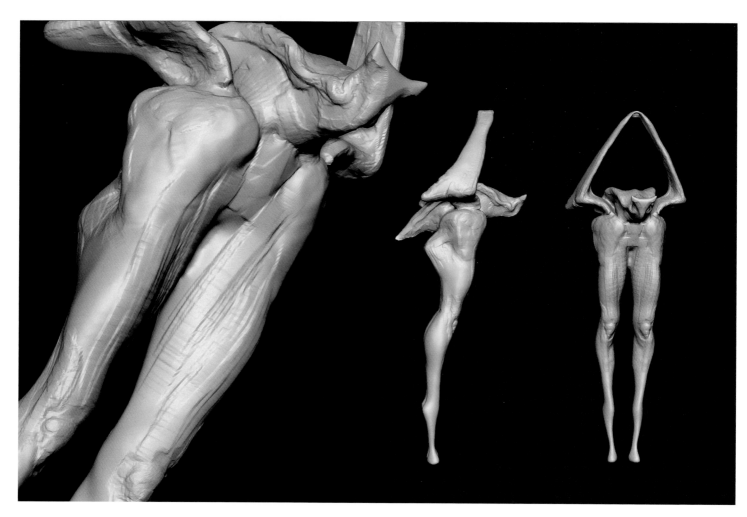

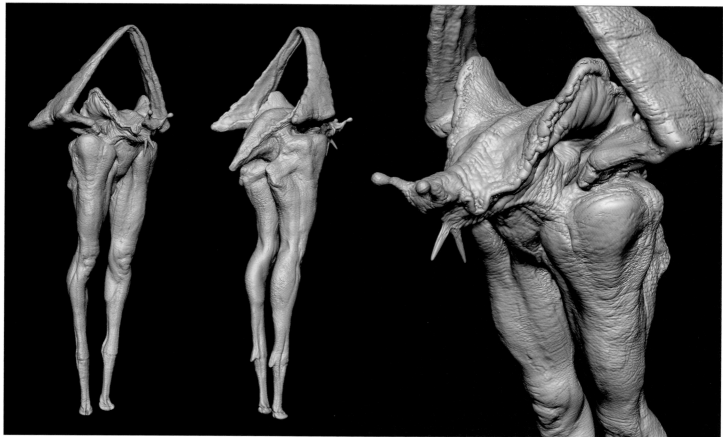

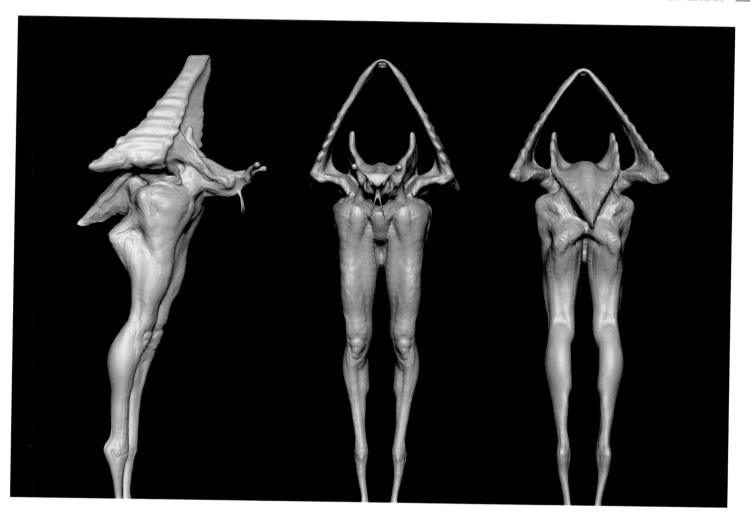

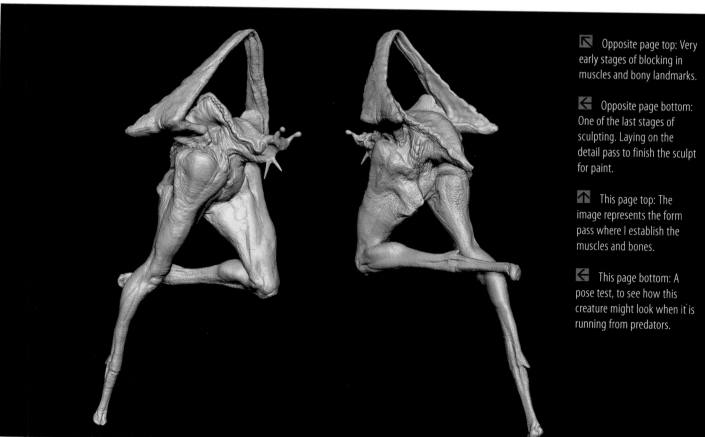

◤ Opposite page top: Very early stages of blocking in muscles and bony landmarks.

◤ Opposite page bottom: One of the last stages of sculpting. Laying on the detail pass to finish the sculpt for paint.

◤ This page top: The image represents the form pass where I establish the muscles and bones.

◤ This page bottom: A pose test, to see how this creature might look when it is running from predators.

↑ This page: A test render/pose to help wrap my head around the creature and its movement.

↑ Top: This color pass was meant to mimic frog and other amphibious type textures.

↑ ← Rest of page: Render passses that get composited in Photoshop to create the final image.

↑ Above: A preliminary test render. I was trying to set mood and environment in my scene.

→ Right: The final image.

canis ornitum

Q: What was your end goal when you first started doing this creature?

Like everyone else, my end goal was to make something cool that resonates with the viewer. My goal was to try to execute a creature that was 75 percent mammal and 25 percent plant. So, you can see a lot of the basic shapes and structure of the creature are derived from the mammal aspect, while the interior shapes reflect more of the plant aspects. The task/challenge for me was to combine these aspects in a cohesive manner that not only seems to legitimately make sense but looks cool as well.

Q: What went through your mind when you looked at the Creature Matrix?

When I began a lot of my creatures, I kept randomly clicking on the matrix; there were so many great ideas that came out of it. However, I ignored a lot of them because I think I knew in my head, right from the start, what I wanted to do for my creatures. In the end, the matrix provided more of a framework for laying out the functions of my creatures.

Q: Where did your initial inspiration come from?

My initial inspiration for this creature, and the majority of my inspiration for my creatures, comes from scribbling random thumbnails in my sketchbooks. I like to draw random squiggles and such and see if I can make something out of them. Sort of like finding order in chaos. I wouldn't call myself a gifted drawer by any means, so I rely on happy accidents a lot of the time. Sort of like when you were a child and looked at the clouds as you lay in the grass … I always tried to see different dinosaurs and faces in the randomness of the clouds. I guess that's the closest analogy I can make to what I do in my sketchbook.

Q: How do you imagine your creature moves or sounds? Did this influence how it developed?

As I worked on this guy, the plan was to make it a whale-faced plant monster. As I developed him further it turned into more of a panther-inspired creature, a stalker-type predator. His design is very thin from the front so most animals/prey would never even see him coming. He moves very slowly through the forest while hunting, not making a peep. When attacking, he accelerates to very high speeds but cannot hold it for too long as his lungs are compressed to help with his camouflage. I always imagined this creature making really high-pitched shrills when it kills something – calling its young to feast on the kill and warding off any lower predators.

Q: How many variations did you do and what directions did you go in to achieve the end result?

There were not too many variations. I had an idea very early on. Most of what I develop I try to see in my head first and then knock it out in 3D once I feel I have a grasp of what I am trying to achieve.

Q: If this creature is a predator, what specific ideas did you have for it in the way it stalks its prey?

As I stated earlier, it is a stalking predator and its camouflage comes in the form of the leaves that form on the outer part of its skin. The leaves wilt and shed and change color with the coming seasons; this way the creature is never caught out of its element and it is perfectly camouflaged into its surroundings all the time. All of these things together make it a very skilled hunter. But, if it is seen from the side, it is easily noticed and doesn't have enough energy to carry on a long chase.

Q: What process did you use for deciding which of your concepts to take forward to a final design?

My general process for selecting which creature to take to final usually comes at the block in stage. I like to hit a bunch of ideas in 3D and see what they look like in space. Sketches are cool and all but they don't always translate to 3D the way you might expect. So for me, it's very important that a creature demands attention in space and looks interesting from all angles.

← Left: The first pen sketch I made, trying to whip up something interesting to work with. I threw a little guy in there for some scale.

↓ Below: The initial block in stage. You can see by the silhouetted shapes that my focus here was on the entire object, not the interior shapes.

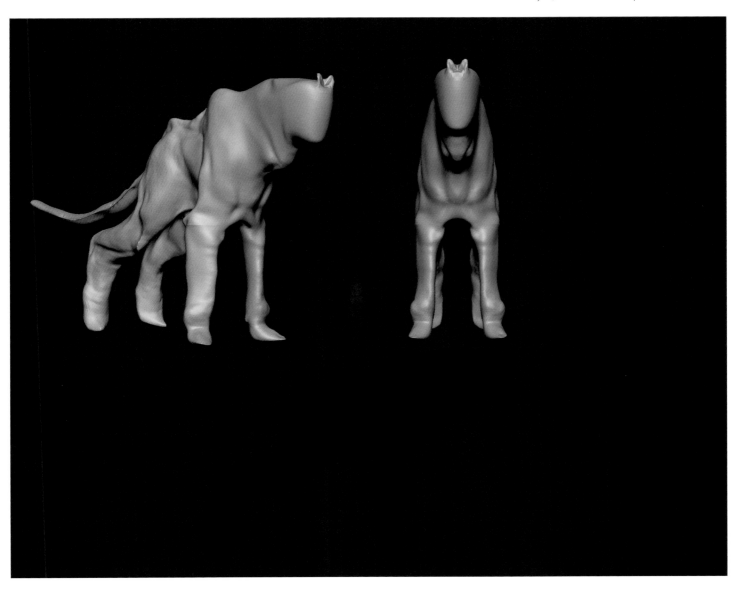

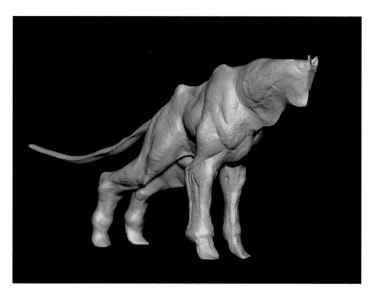

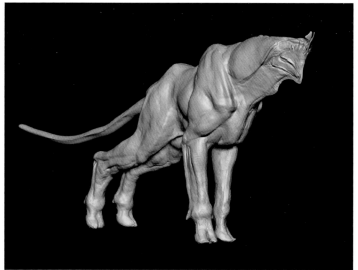

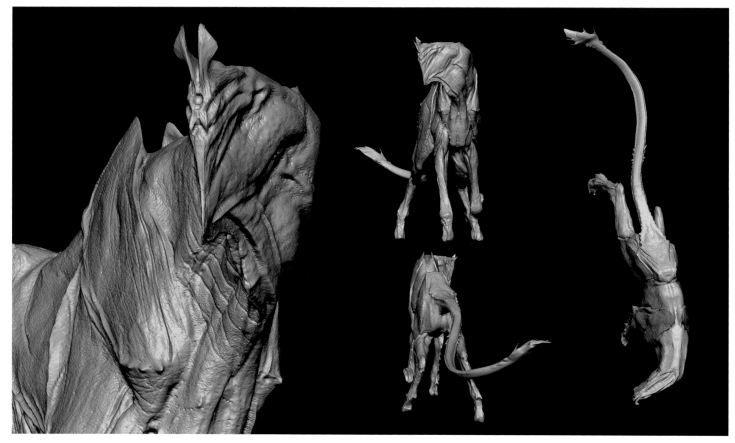

Q: **What did you try in terms of markings/fur/hair/ hide/teeth?**

I tried making this creature with fur and stuff early on but it didn't have the punch that I wanted. It also made him feel too soft to be a predator. I gave him a big red Cyclops-like eye; I felt that smacking this eye on the front of its face really added to the predator vibe and lets the viewer know that all this creature does is hunt. The inspiration for the mouth came from those little staple-remover things that have the four teeth to pull staples from paper. They always look aggressive to me, so I thought I'd give it a try.

⬆ Top images: These images show my workflow in developing and refining the interior forms and structure of the creature.

⬆ Above: Final detail pass, to add more visual interest and to support the larger forms.

↑ Above: I layered in some brighter colors to work with. I find it easier to pull it back in Photoshop than to try to punch the color later.

← Left: Early pose to consider how this creature might fill the space/environment.

⬆ Above images: Layers of the render that I manipulate and overlay on top of each other to achieve the final image to the right.

➔ Right: The final image.

other concepts

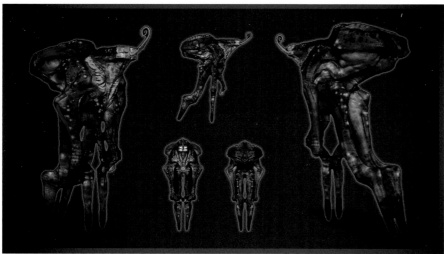

Nektar Lingent

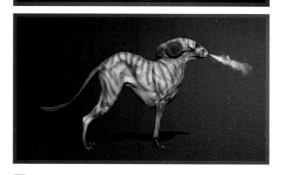

Supersoaker

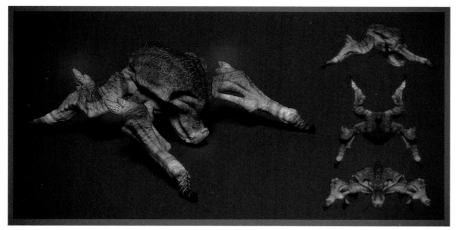

Seedsucka   Geosaurus

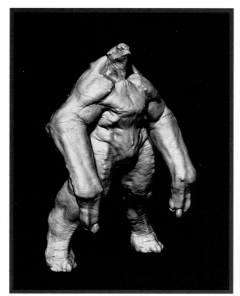

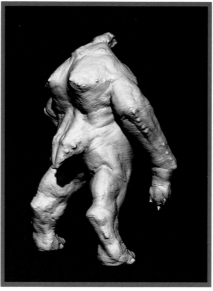

Untitled

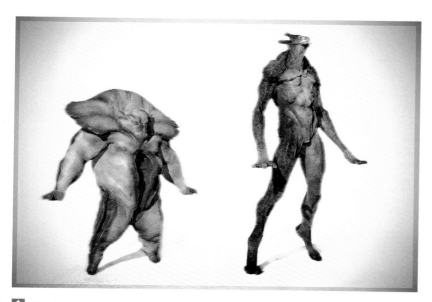

 Bipeds

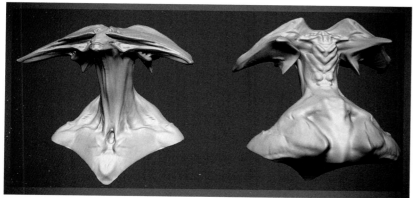

⬆ Untitled   ⬇ Untitled

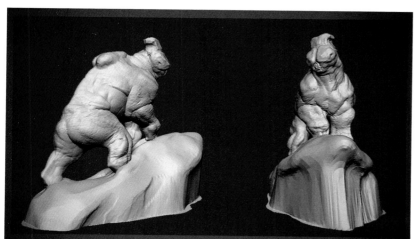

These sketches, speed sculpts and designs are ideas that didn't
make it past the early ideation stage, but present exciting would-be
creatures and concepts to explore in the future.

⬆ Untitled

⬆ Untitled

⬆ Bovibara

⬆ Wetlands Sifter

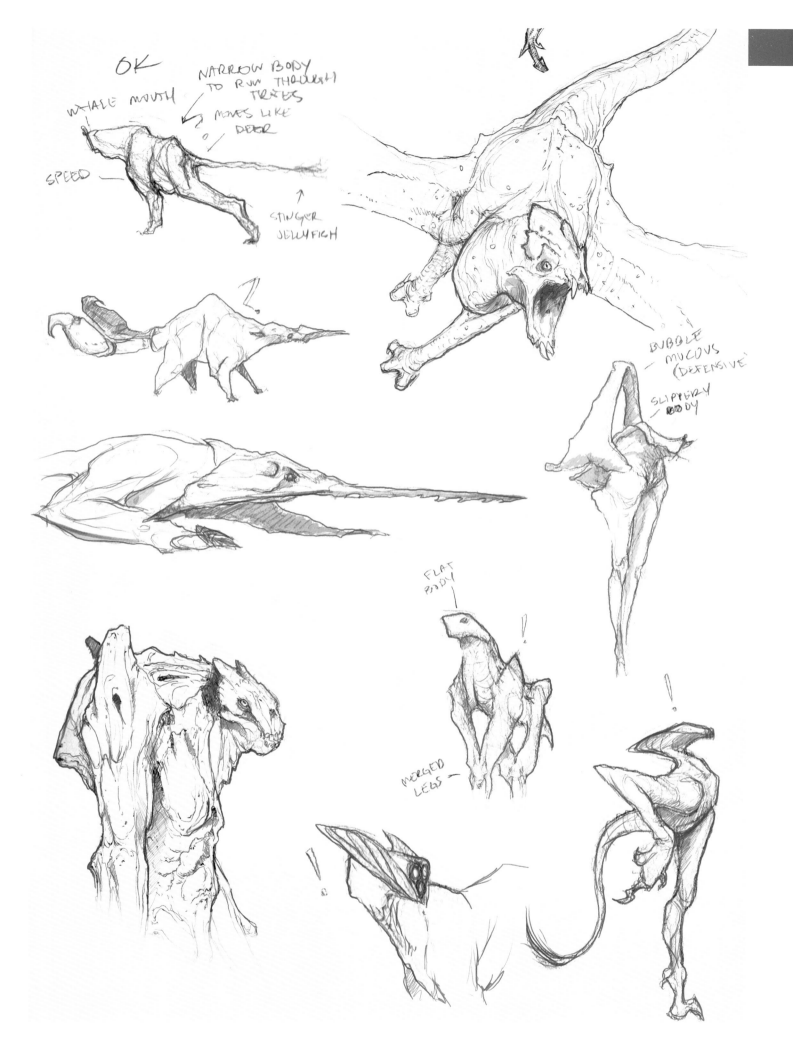

OK

WHALE MOUTH

NARROW BODY
TO RUN THROUGH
TREES

MOVES LIKE
DEER

SPEED

STINGER
JELLYFISH

BUBBLE
MUCOUS
(DEFENSIVE)

SLIPPERY
BODY

FLAT
BODY

MERGED
LEGS

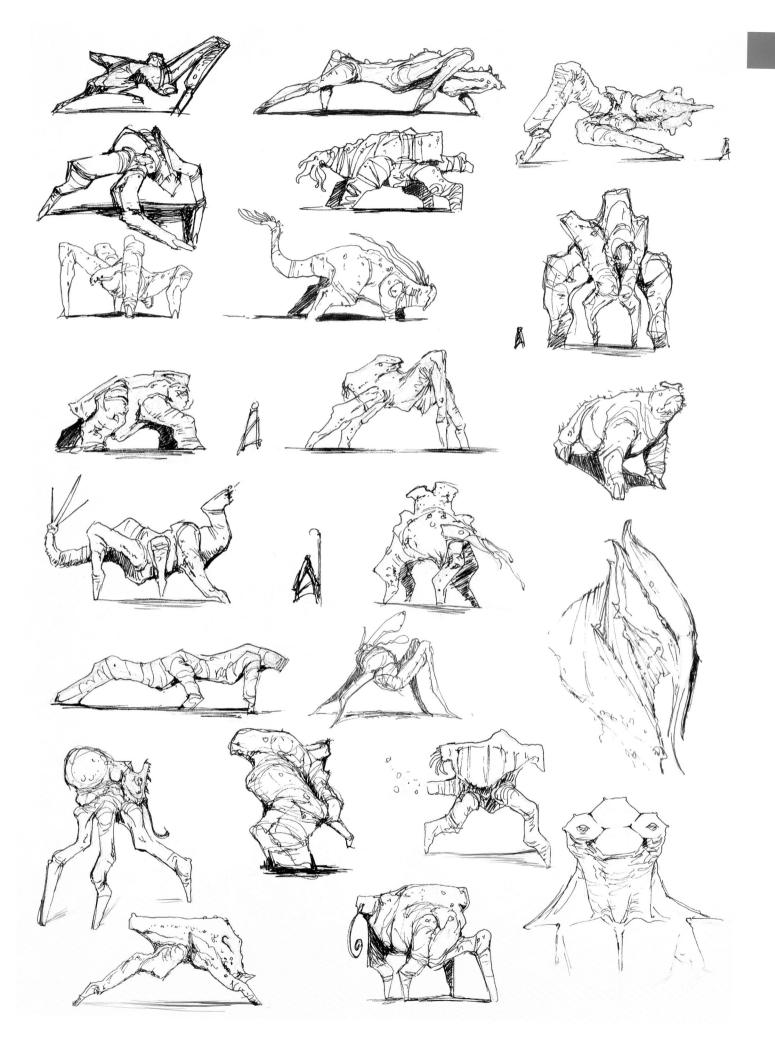

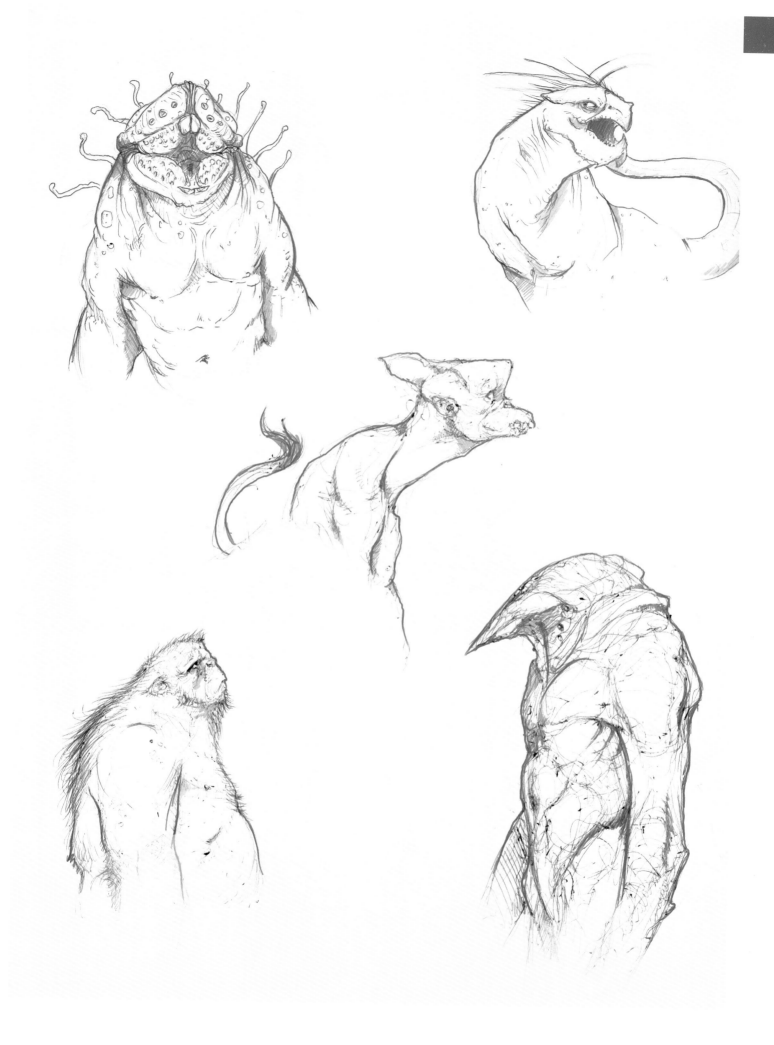

josh herman .

I have always been inspired by art, even as a kid. I drew a lot and took as many art classes as I could (mostly because they were more fun), but during and after high school I never thought about art as a career. After high school I took some time off from school and tried some other things. Eventually I ended up going to a local school in Colorado where I studied animation.

After this, I wanted to continue my education and so decided to attend the Gnomon School of Visual Effects, which was probably the start of my 'big break'. All of the teachers there were professional, working artists, and I was surrounded by lots of students with great work ethics, and it was easy to get to know people. During my time there, we went on tours of some of the local studios, including Legacy Effects during my last term. I asked them to look at my portfolio. After a solid recommendation and some lucky timing, I was hired right after I graduated.

I don't have anyone I would call a mentor specifically, but I have a few artist friends who I respect a lot and will go to for advice. Bryan and Ian, two of the other artists featured in this book, have become good friends and I refer to them all the time in this way.

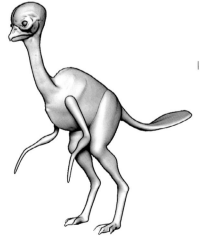

I currently work at Marvel Studios, working on the Marvel Cinematic Universe movies like *Avengers, Iron Man 3, Thor: The Dark World, Captain America: The Winter Solider, Guardians of the Galaxy*, and now on *Avengers 2*. A typical day for me can vary. Some days I will be concepting characters or creatures, other days I will be modeling some from an existing design, which is the case for characters like Iron Man. Other times I might be doing R&D for the way a character moves, or I might be working on look development.

I'm a huge gamer. I love playing all types of games – video, board, RPG. I'm also a big movie buff and love most things sci-fi and the action movies from the 1980s and 1990s. I also like to do my own personal art and I enjoying teaching classes. I taught a ZBrush class at CDA in Pasadena and I currently teach an online workshop at CGWorkshops on Hard Surface Character Modeling.

The best advice I think I can give an emerging artist is to develop a good work ethic, take every opportunity you can get your hands on, and, most importantly, be nice. The industry is small and you never know who you will meet or work with again. A lot of new and young artists can come off as over-confident right when they get out of school. So, be nice, be humble and if you get a shot, take it because it's competitive out there.

In terms of the challenges facing CG artists working in the industry today, many people would probably say 'outsourcing' or something that relates to the long hours that a lot of CG people work. But a wider problem, in my opinion, is that CG artists are only just now starting to refer to themselves as artists. For a while now we have been regarded as just someone who 'works on a computer' and the computer is what does the artwork, which is obviously completely false. Because of that, we often aren't given the credit that we deserve. Along with that, everyone with a computer now has access to programs like Photoshop, and because they can use the program at home they may underestimate the amount of work and time it takes to become a professional artist.

Right now I'm really not sure what lays ahead for me. I love my job, and I love the movies that I work on and the team I work with, so I'm happy. Maybe one day way down the line I'd like to develop my own stories for movies or games, but not right now.

red-finned slark

JOSH HERMAN

Q: **What was your end goal when you first started designing this creature?**

I wanted to design a mean water creature. Initially I was looking at animals like honey badgers that are just mean and angry, with not a whole lot of common sense. This creature lives in the water and it does not care about anything else other than food, so its entire focus is that. Also, I wanted to do something relatively simple design wise … I wanted to play around with different options within a simple design.

Q: **Did you get this idea from the Creature Matrix or did you have something preconceived?**

Yes, this idea came from the Creature Matrix. I looked at the matrix list and picked out some things I thought were interesting. I knew I wanted to do something in the water. After I chose water, I picked out other traits that I thought would be fun – I chose 'omnivore', 'flippers' and 'speed'. Making a creature that is really fast and eats anything was appealing to me.

Q: **It's great how you incorporated the flipper into the tail section – you can tell that this body design would make it a fast mover.**

Initially, in my very first sculpt, I basically created an underwater badger, but I felt like it needed more as it didn't really feel aquatic. If you look at animals that live underwater, like crocodiles and frogs, you see they don't really have a neck but instead their head goes straight into their body. So I started incorporating those kinds of shapes, to give it that aquatic feel, mirroring the animals you see underwater.

Q: **One of the coolest things you posted with your image is a goofy, deformed photo of you, which leads to a question about your initial inspiration for this creature. You have talked a bit about the badger, but where does this photo come into play in terms of inspiration?**

This photo (see page 174) is from Photobooth on my iPad. I was just playing around with it and making weird faces. I took a picture that pretty much looked like my creature – with a tiny mouth and big, buggy eyes. When I was doing this, I was opening my mouth and it reminded me of when an animal is eating – when it's so zoned in on feeding that its eyes bug out and glaze over, and all it focuses on is eating, nothing else. This is what I wanted to capture in my creature. I just ran with it from there, and starting morphing it and taking a bit of inspiration from a frog and a badger.

Q: **How did you imagine your creature moving or sounding, and did this influence how you developed it? Was there a particular way that you imagined it would swim underwater?**

I was thinking it would be a sprinter rather than a marathon runner … it is not built to go for long distances but for short, compact bursts of speed. It sits and waits and as soon as it sees something, it goes after it. Also, I made it a mammal because I wanted it to have that kind of feel as well, so it could maybe crawl on land for a while and chill out, like a crocodile (even though that's not a mammal!)

Q: **Did you do many variations when you first started this? Did you do any pencil sketches?**

No, I don't tend to work with pencil sketches. Instead I start with one sculpture and then evolve it slowly. I will just rough something out and then let the design start to guide itself. Sometimes I might have an interesting reference, maybe a cool photo or an idea from a friend. I don't draw very well so I find it easier to rough out a sculpture first. So for this guy, one of my WIP shots (see page opposite) looks almost like an evolutionary chart where it slowly changes from the first sculpt to later ones. From beginning to end it's different but not too different – so my initial idea stayed intact.

Q: **You said that this creature is omnivorous so it could be eating animals just as much as it would be eating plants. How did you see it hunting its**

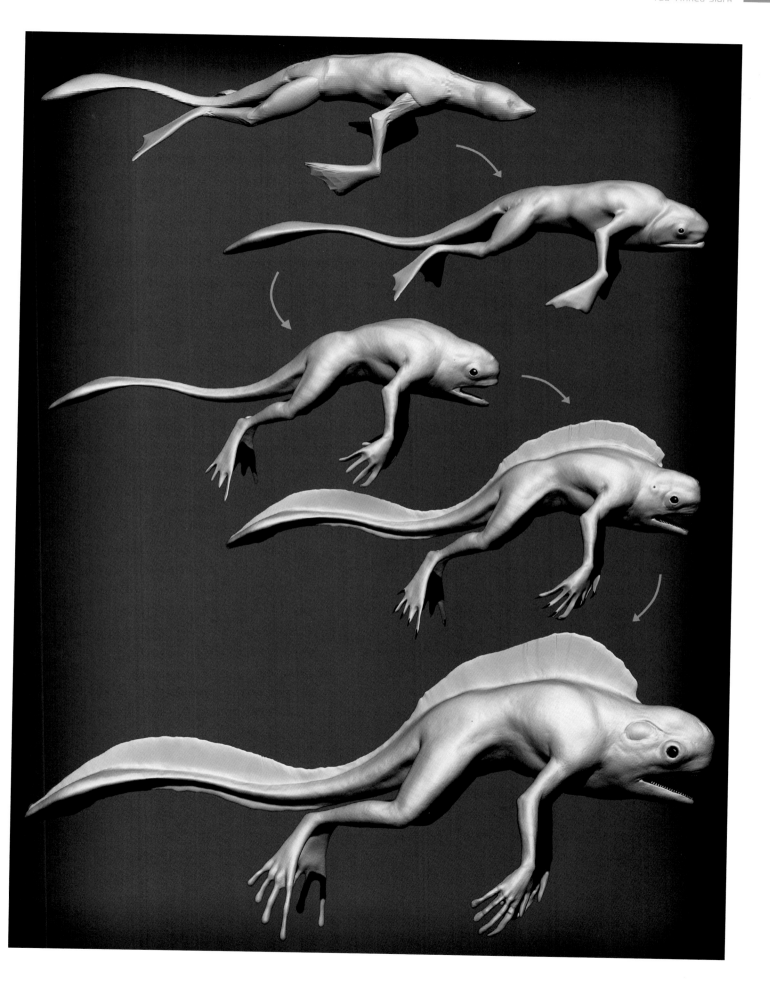

prey? You did a really cool image of a little fish creature, which looks like a guppy ... How did you imagine your creature hunting this little guy?

I see my creature mostly hunting other animals, but if it got really hungry and there was no other available food, it would eat plants, garbage or maybe even coral and rocks. It's kind of like a goat – it will eat the best meal it can get. The little fish you refer to is actually a baby version of my creature. I think the babies would be really vulnerable; these guys are pretty ruthless and if they saw the babies, they would eat them. They have no connection to them. In terms of how it hunts its prey, I imagine it hiding out, not necessarily camouflaged, but maybe dwelling in a cave, hiding in the background until it can strike and jump out at its prey.

Q: So you considered some color variations. What was your thought process behind those?

Almost all of the color variations are based on actual animals. I wanted to try some different colors to see what they felt like. Some of the creatures have an amphibian feel, some are more swampy, some are tropical. Just playing with the color made a pretty big difference to where I can see them living. The green camo one is inspired by a toad or a swamp salamander, the one below that is like a green fish or frog, the purple one at the bottom is a tropical fish, and the red, white and black one is not really based on any animal but more intended to be a graphic shape.

Early on I had an idea that I want to create a dynamic image for the final – a group shot with a bunch of them swarming around some prey. Because of this, the color choice became really important. If I went for something with a complex pattern it would have been much harder to balance the illustration. There would have been so many lines and so much difference in contrast and value that the final image might have been harder to read. So going with something that has one color from the tip of the head to the end of the tail makes it easier to follow and see a character, and creates lines that can point you through the illustration, guiding your eye.

Continued on page 176…

Left: Inspirational self-portrait from my iPad.

Below images: Preliminary color test in Keyshot. This was used to check if the forms were reading well, and to test how the colors and lighting would look. Bottom: Color variations in ZBrush for the final color scheme. The different colors show that the Slark could fit in many environments.

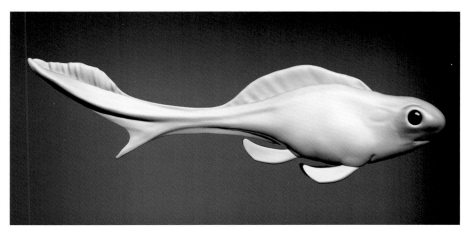

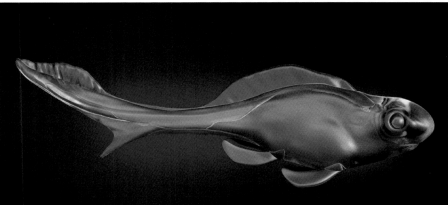

⬆ Above: A tiny squid, aka food for the Slark, used for reference in the final composition.

⬅◥ Left and above left: Sculpt for the baby Red-finned Slark.

⬇ Below: Side 'beauty shot' of the Slark. I would use something like this to show the design to clients. It's simple and not distracting.

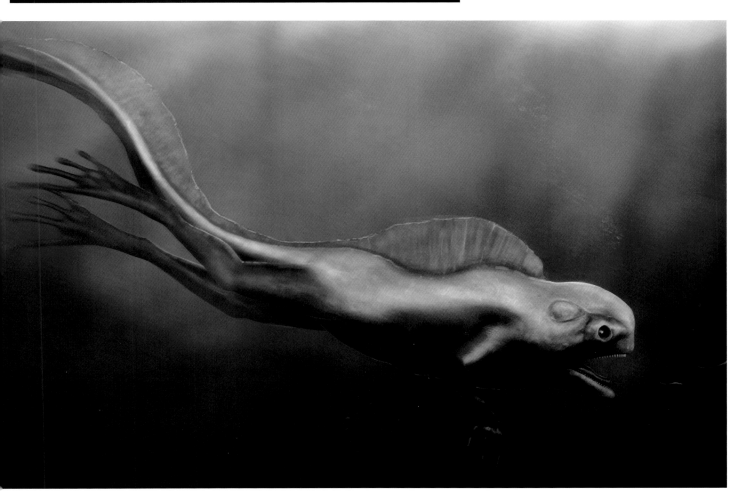

Q: **Was the dynamic shot at the end the most challenging part of this project?**

Yeah, I think it was. I spent a lot of time on the composition of that, starting with just the black-and-white image that you see, the first test. Without thinking about composition at all I just posed five or six different versions of this guy, by themselves without combining them, and then I brought them all into one final and started to put them next to each other to see which angles complemented each other. Once I found those, I started thinking about what angles would look good for that specific composition. Once I got that, then I started getting the composition going, so playing with which character would be in front or would they all be in front – trying to find a way to create a shape for the characters. Then I moved from that to paint-over, kind of a loose sketchy thing, with more color in it. That was to add more dynamics to it, tilting to camera, and cutting some characters out of frame so it didn't feel so perfectly cropped. It took a long time.

Q: **Just so it feels a bit more natural...**

Yes. I was also trying to create a nice flow through the piece so you can look at multiple things and not feel like there is only one thing to focus on. It's not just one character, it's a bunch of them, so I wanted each of them to have their own interest. I also tried to play with the negative space in the center of the composition – to make that an interesting shape that aids in guiding your eye around and helps you look at everything. I spent a long time experimenting and trying things out. Sometimes when you're making a design, you're making it for something specific. This design was made for this image, so while some of the other color options are more interesting and maybe 'cooler', I don't think they would work as well for this image.

Q: **You have that extra layer of the composition as well...**

Which kind of goes into the images showing the creature from the side – one of it diving and one of the baby (see previous page). If you have both of these images, and if I was presenting them to a director or a client, I'd say the diving one is the image I would present first because it is more of a beauty shot to show off the design, but it also shows the

entire character. The side view is intended to clearly show what the character looks like … there is no story or crazy composition going on. It's just a simple view of the character. Even the little guys he's chasing are blurred and not important to the image.

Above: Initial 3D block out. Here I was playing with poses and the idea that a group of slarks were swarming around one last piece of food.

Above: After the block out, I did a paint-over to try to push the composition as well as colors and mood.

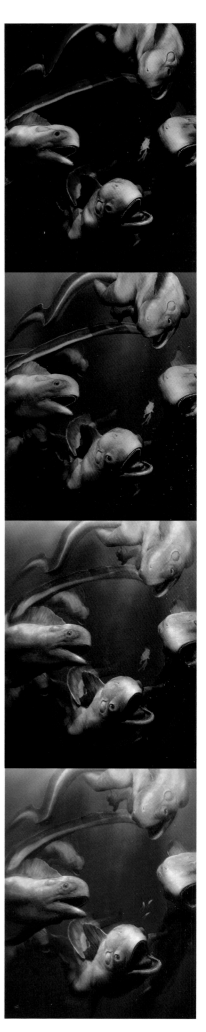

Above: ZBrush render passes used to make the final illustration.

Right column: Process of the final composition.

Opposite page: The final image.

eater of worlds

JOSH HERMAN

Q: What was your end goal for this creature?

I wanted to do something that no one else was going to do. I wanted to do something big. When we were brainstorming for this book, we were talking about different types of predators and prey, and I thought that doing an apex predator sounded pretty cool. I thought about the ultimate apex predator – something that nothing else hunts. The only thing that kills it is age or not finding food. So I decided to do something that was so big that it could eat entire planets – there's nothing else as massive. It doesn't have anything that can even compare to it in size. I pulled some inspiration from jellyfish and squid, and thought about bioluminescence. I wanted something that was in space, in a way camouflaging itself in space with bioluminescence.

Q: You went to the top of the food chain in the universe … Did you give any thought to where this creature came from? Is this something mythological, almost like a god? What is its back story?

I hadn't entirely thought about its back story too much until recently. I like the idea of it being the only one of its kind. I did some research on things that can live in space, and the only things I found were some really small bugs called water bears. They've been tested by scientists and put in vacuums in space and survived, and have also been frozen and heated to volcanic-type heats. They can survive anything. I like the idea that there is something out in space that has evolved to grow bigger and bigger, and has been around for a couple of millennia, getting bigger and bigger, feeding off whatever nutrients it can find. It's probably the only one that exists. I don't imagine it laying eggs or having a mate or anything like that. Because of its size, unless it lays eggs in space or on a planet, it doesn't really have an environment to do that in.

Q: Tell me about your initial inspiration/s.

Initially I really liked the idea of it being squid-like, and that it ingests and eat planets, almost holding them in its stomach. The planet doesn't have a chance to fight back – it is swallowed whole, which is what a squid does with its prey. I looked at a lot of cephalopods and jellyfish, studying their shapes. For scale there is nothing that big so it was really hard to find references. Mostly I looked at a lot of underwater creatures … some of the most terrifying things I can think of existing would be really deep underwater or out in space. Both environments have extreme pressures and temperatures and no air. So underwater creatures were a natural reference for my space creature.

Q: How does this creature move throughout the galaxy? Did you get inspired in terms of its movement through the squid and the cephalopods?

Actually, no. It's kind of a disgusting creature. It absorbs whatever nutrients it can find, it swallows them and then goes into a hibernation mode. I was reading about underwater bugs that hibernate for 10 years at time, until something comes into contact with them, then they wake up. So this creature would absorb a planet and then sleep for a long time, maintaining as much of that energy as possible. The reason I didn't use squids and cephalopods as references for my creature's movement is that the creature is in space and has no resistance (like the squid has in water). So I looked at NASA and how they control their ships in space. They have lots of little boosters on the sides of their ships to land them on the moon and things. So I thought this creature could have three or four little orifices where it emits gas (farts) and balances itself out (like a ship does). It doesn't have to do this very often, though, because when it goes into hibernation mode it takes all of its chemicals and stretches out its tentacles as far as it can – so when it's floating around in space it's like a web. When one of the tentacles touches something, it wakes up, adjusts, eats it, then goes back to sleep.

Q: Did you do any thumbnails or sketches after you gathered your references?

Most of my creatures I start in 3D. When I started this one, I had a basic shape in mind. I knew I wanted this creature's

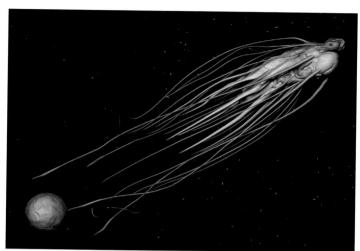

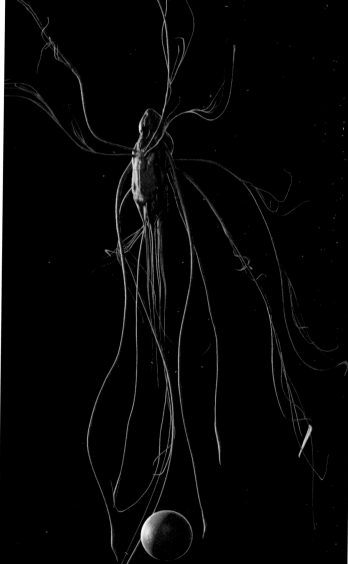

⬆ Above: Initial block out based mostly on jellyfish.

⬈ Top right: My second pass. Here I was referencing squid and octopus anatomy.

➡ Right: Lighting test in Keyshot. I also used this to play with compositions and scale.

mouthparts to protrude out of it and envelop planets. I didn't do any sketches at all. One of the challenges I had was trying to see what the character would look like with tentacles, and doing this in 3D. There are so many pieces to it, it's not all one piece … this thing has probably 60 plus tentacles. It retrospect I probably should have done some sketches to see overall some of the shapes. Halfway through I had to start freestyling it.

Is this creature male or female?

It's asexual.

Almost like a microorganism but just the largest thing in the galaxy?

I think of it as a really big mite, like a dust mite. It's the only one of its kind, so even if it has a gender, no one is going to know anyway.

Did you get stuck at any point?

At one point I had a silhouette blocked out and I crudely roughed it in, and all of a sudden I knew what I wanted shape-wise and then had to take everything I'd done and rebuild it all for it to start working. I wanted to have overlaps to see what was on the inside and outside. Initially I did it all from one mesh, except for the tentacles, then I wanted to break all of it apart so I could do more with it. At that point I wasn't entirely sure how to approach it. I wasn't really getting stuck, I was just trying to figure out how I was going to approach the next step.

So you came up with this big concept at the beginning, but what was your thought process as you started to hone in on some areas of interest?

Instead of using colors, hair or markings, I tried to show the different areas of the creature – the heart, nerves, brain and eyes – by showing what the materials are. So, for the heart I wanted it to have a chunky, juicy feeling; for the eyes, then the material should be thinner, smoother and translucent; the skin I wanted to feel like skin, and so on.

You've created one of the more intimidating images in the book. Does this character have any sort of weakness? Does Earth stand any chance against it?

No, Earth doesn't stand any chance against it. In one of my initial sketches I had all of these tiny missiles coming from Earth, making a last stand. The missiles are the size of France but compared to the creature, they are tiny. It doesn't have any weakness. It's the top of the food chain. The only thing is that maybe there would be some type of environment on a planet, or black holes, which it can't control.

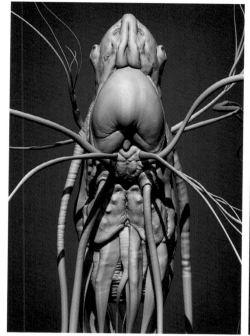 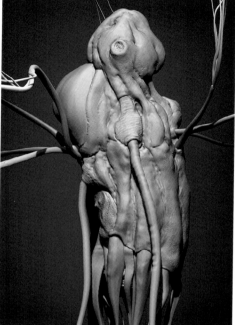 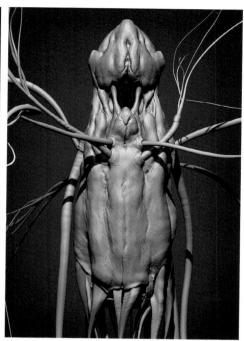

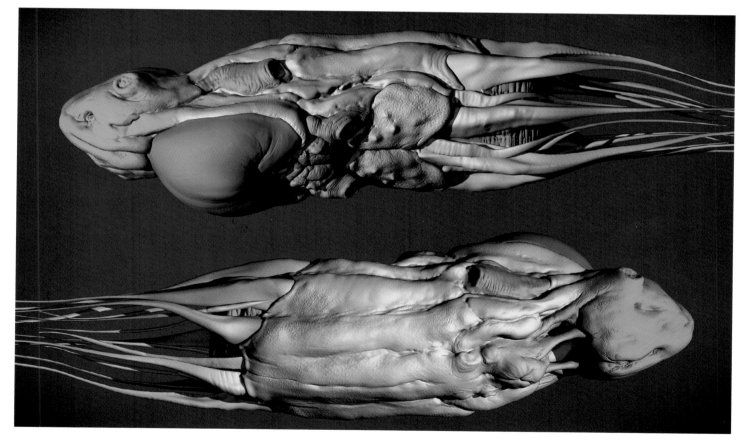

↖ Opposite page: Early lighting test in Keyshot, playing with scale.

↑ Top row: Final body sculpt.
↑ Above: Anatomy of the Eater of Worlds:
Green = brain center
Blue = visual cortex
Red = major pulmonary systems
Yellow = nerve bundle
Purple = mouth
Pink = primary tentacle connections
Orange = gas emitters

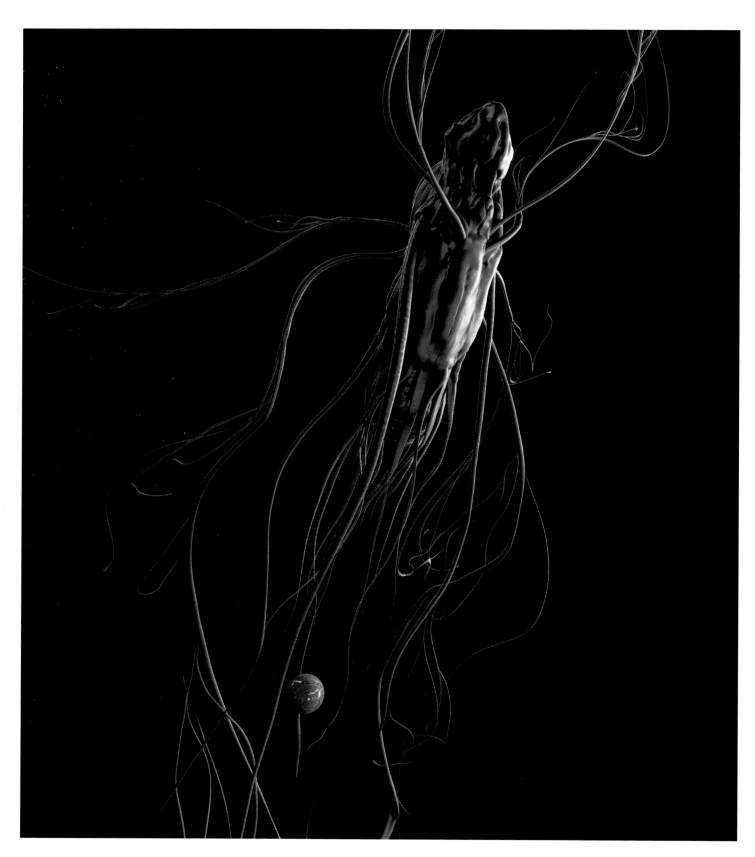

↑ This page: Final sculpt rendered in Keyshot, before cropping and paint-over in Photoshop.

↗ Opposite page: The final image.

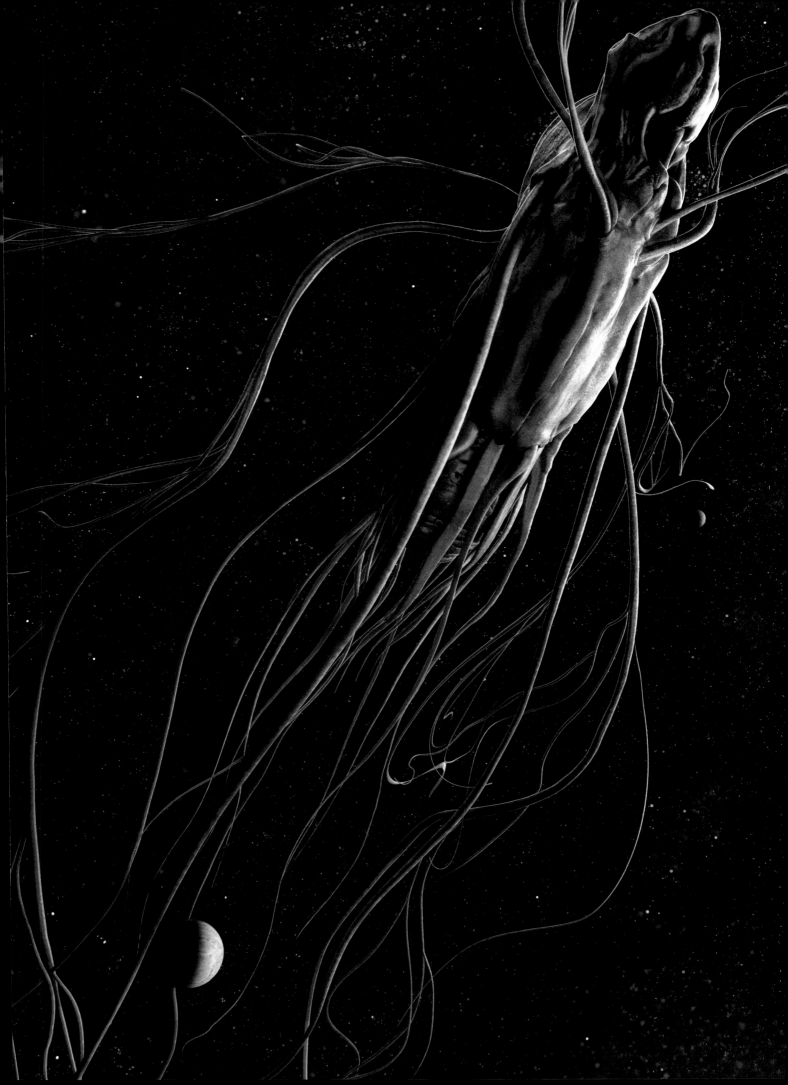

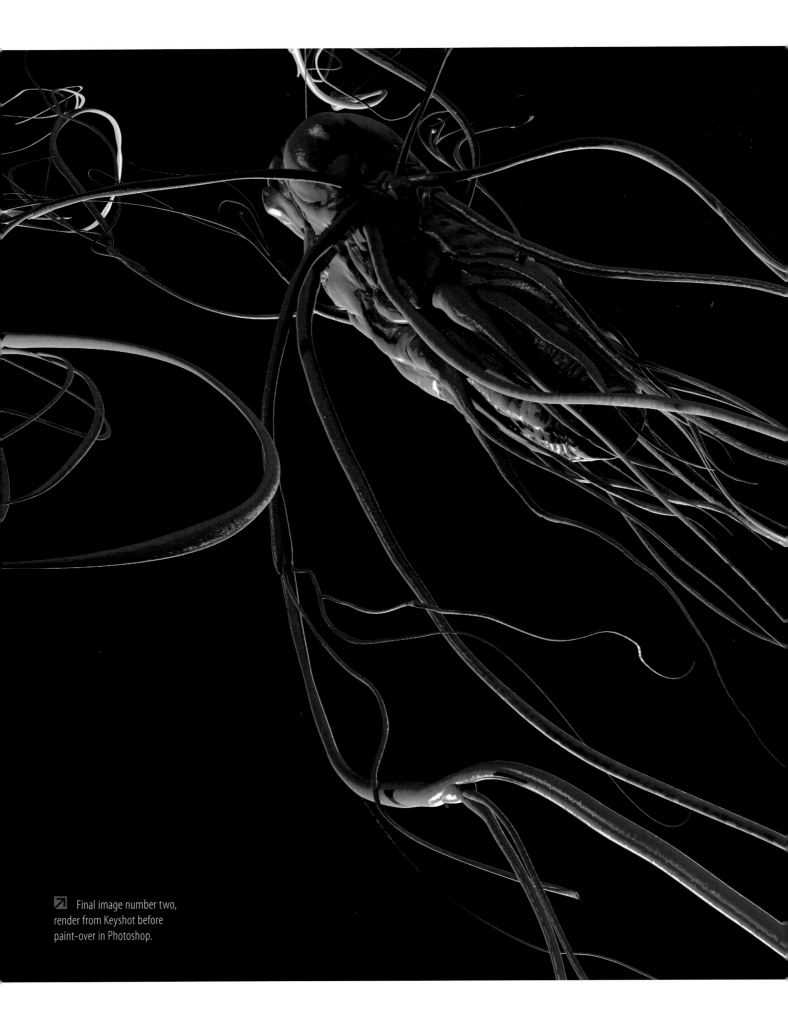

Final image number two, render from Keyshot before paint-over in Photoshop.

monster puppy

JOSH HERMAN

Q: Tell us a little bit about what inspired this creature…

In a quick, bad decision during the last three weeks of the deadline of this book, right when I was trying to cram to get some images done, we decided to get a puppy. I love him and he's super cute and adorable but he's also full of energy and whenever he's awake he'll literally eat whatever he can find. We put him outside and he was eating dirt, he'll also eat plastic, metal, glass – anything he can get his mouth around. He only cares about that.

Also, he was waking up two to three times minimum a night, and I was on deadline and extremely sleep-deprived. Some nights I stayed up late working till midnight or later and then he'd wake up at 2 am, 4 am, 6 am and 8 am, then I'd have to be at work at 9 am. After the first week, or the first two to three days, of sleep deprivation, I thought, "I kind of hate you … you're super cute but I kind of hate you!" So I started to have this mental image of him – a monstrous version of him, which was also informed by your typical werewolf.

The sculpt evolution was pretty quick … immediately when I blocked it in he was looking a little ape-like so I tried to push some of the bug-eyed, flatter-faced, rounder-mouthed things he has, and added some wrinkles. I liked that it was a goofier take on him, but he still had a little monstrous feel to him.

Q: Some of the most effective creatures, even if they're meant to be horrific or monstrous, have a little bit of humor to them, too. This one definitely does that. What did you experiment with in terms of the color and patterns?

I was just interpreting him as a werewolf … like if he was a monster in the shape of a human, werewolf-style, what would he look like. I took patterns from him, I took pictures of him, and used some of them for the comp. He would always sleep on my lap or sleep next to me – when he was actually asleep and not eating things – and I would reference him, so his eyes are the same, the patterns on his mouth and chest … I really did just try to reinterpret him as much as possible. I thought it was a fun last thing to do, in the last two weeks of the book's deadline. At the time of trying to meet this deadline, he was the creature of my nightmares.

Q: So for all the horrific, crazy monsters in the book that could be haunting your dreams, your nightmare creature is a just a cute little puppy…

Yes, this is the one that scares me the most!

Q: So pencil sketches don't really apply here…

No, it was a super quick one. The inspiration was all from one place – my puppy – and from werewolves.

My adorable French bulldog puppy, Spock. Not in monster form.

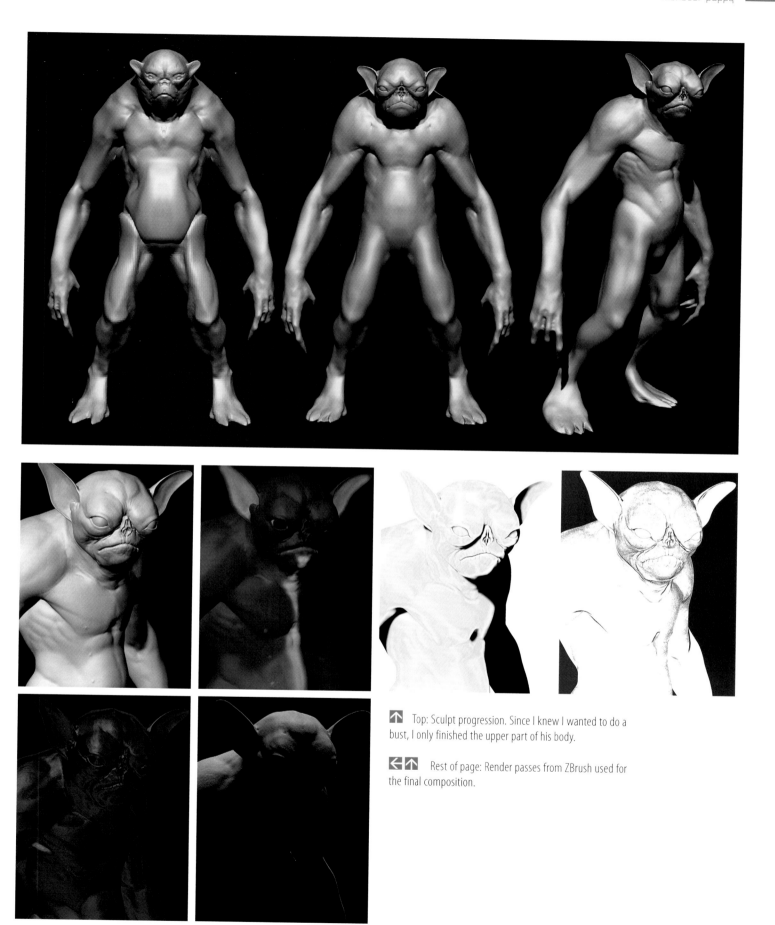

⬆ Top: Sculpt progression. Since I knew I wanted to do a bust, I only finished the upper part of his body.

⬅⬆ Rest of page: Render passes from ZBrush used for the final composition.

→ Right: Initial render from ZBrush before compositing and paint-over in Photoshop.

↘ Below: Near final image after paint-over.

→ Opposite page: Fully formed monster puppy.

swamp golem

JOSH HERMAN

Q: **What was your end goal when creating this creature?**

My goal changed. At the beginning I wanted to make a gaseous creature that emits poison and lives in a swamp or jungle. Then it evolved and I wanted to play with the idea that this creature wouldn't actually emit gas, but, with its humanoid anatomy, instead of using muscles and bone to move it moves by transferring the gas from one part of its body to another. It's very much like a hydraulic set-up, an air-powered creature.

Q: **Why did you choose for it to have a humanoid anatomy?**

It was mostly for fun. I wanted to try it and see what it would look like, and also if could I make it different enough that you can read it as not totally human. I don't know if it's as successful as I was hoping, but that was at least the challenge.

Q: **What was the most difficult part in creating this creature?**

The shapes came together pretty quickly but the hardest part was probably figuring out how I wanted to present it – the composition and the rendering and how I should show this character. I wasn't entirely sure if I wanted it to be moving and changing shape all the time because how do you present that? Because of that limitation, I changed the idea a little bit … so maybe that is how he moves but he doesn't move a lot as it takes a lot of energy for him to move … he just hangs out in the swamp in the water and absorbs nutrients through the water and the air. The hardest part was how to show that.

Q: **Did you do any pencil sketches in your development or was it just a ZBrush flow?**

It was pretty much just a ZBrush flow. I wanted to use ZRemesher with this guy, to do something that had some big concaves in it and some big overlaps, and see how

ZRemesher would deal with it – and it did really good. So I started working with it and went from there.

Q: **It seems almost all the initial development stuff is happening in ZBrush now…**

Yes, it's amazing to see how quickly you can block out a creature. Obviously if you're great at sketching and thumbnails in Photoshop or on paper, that's a huge skill … but it's not a big time-intensive process to block something out in ZBrush or Sculptris or any of the sculpting packages anymore, so it doesn't take you that long. In 15 or 30 minutes you can have something that's pretty well refined and represents the shapes you want from all angles.

Q: **When it comes to the color on this creature, you have a shot showing the process … the color has shifted from the grey-blues and purples into the very green that you went with. Did you find yourself doing a lot of discovery when it came to the colors?**

No, actually. In each of my creatures for the book I had a vision of what I wanted to try. For my Red-finned Slark I wanted to have a dynamic composition with stark colors; with my Eater of Worlds I wanted to play with scale and do something in space. With this one I wanted to try to do something that was monochromatic and play with something with a lot of greens and then see how I could guide the eye. I started trying to add in some swirling around him in the water, with some smoke and atmosphere, so hopefully there's a bit of a flow to it. It was mostly because I wanted the challenge of creating a character that's almost entirely one color.

Q: **The close-up shot is really effective in that you have a lot of subtle things happening, but it is very monochromatic when you first look at it. Then, when you look closer, you see some purples and subtly played-up colors…**

In a lot of courses you'll hear that simple form and complex

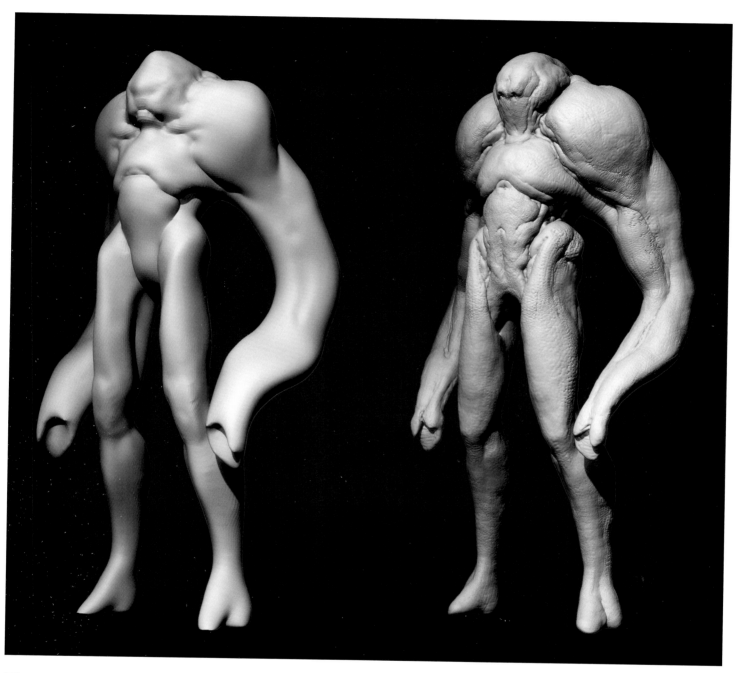

ZBrush sculpt progression. Initial sketch to final sculpt.

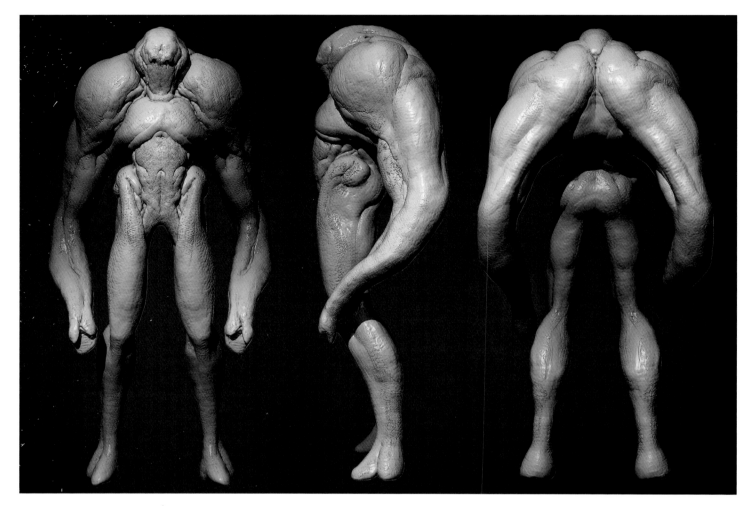

color are a recipe you can use for creature design. For this creature and on the Red-finned Slark, I didn't want to do that. With the Slark I wanted to do something that was more for graphic shape, and use at least two stark colors rather than have a complex pattern. In terms of this creature, if you look at animals, even big animals, most of the time they are one maybe two colors maximum … if you look at sharks and hippos, they are one color but they have variation to them, enough that they are really interesting when you look at them up close or even from far away. I wanted to try something like that.

⬆ Above: Final sculpt.

➡ Opposite page: ZBrush render passes used for compositing the final image.

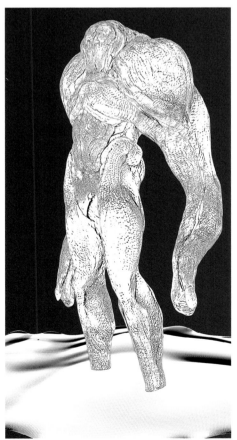

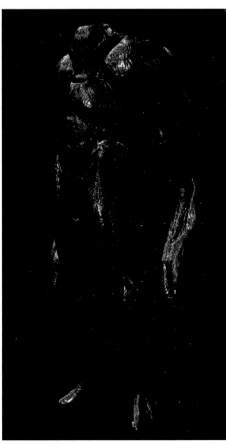

↑→ This page: Final image progress. I started with a full-body shot with the Golem standing in water. In the end, the composition wasn't strong and I focused on a bust.

→ Opposite page: The final image.

martin rezard.

BIOGRAPHY

Photograph credit: Pauline Fowler.

Creating images, characters and creatures has always been a very strong passion of mine, since my early childhood. I started modeling characters in clay when I was 10 or 11 years old, and did my first plaster bandage life cast on my little brother when I was 16. I sculpted a couple of characters on him from this and just kept on going, producing masks and prosthetic make-ups. It was very evident to me from my early teens that I would not be able to hold down a 'normal' job, so I was left with two choices – be a rock star or try my best at being a sculptor/special make-up effects artist. The rock star thing didn't work out so well…

I saw *The Dark Crystal* at the cinema when it came out, and it was a huge shock to me to witness this totally other worldly universe brought to life in such a vivid and convincing manner through the talent and dedication of a group of gifted individuals. It was an absolute revelation to me and illuminated a bright path towards where I wanted to go, what I wanted to do with my life.

Greystoke, Star Wars, Gremlins, The Howling, Explorers, Little Shop of Horrors, and most of the films coming out at that time were a constant inspiration for me; as well as all the films displaying the work of Ray Harryhausen. In France, we also had at the time a very creative flow of graphic novels coming from the brilliant minds of such artists as Mœbius, Philippe Druillet,

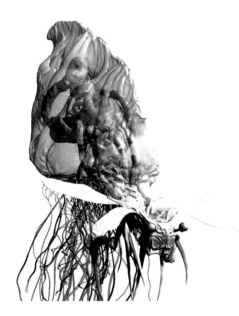

Caza, Bilal, etc., most of whom had their work published in magazines such as *Métal Hurlant*. I have always looked up to Jim Henson, Lyle Conway, Neal Scanlan, Rick Baker, Phil Tippet, Rob Bottin and Steve Johnson, as well as John Coltrane, Angus Young, Eddie Van Halen, Chet Baker, Bobby MC Ferrin, Wayne Shorter, Jacques Cousteau, David Attenborough and Buster Keaton, among others.

I am self-taught, and got my inspiration from books, magazines, movies and sharing experiences with friends with the same passion. I lived on the same street as Jean Christophe Spadaccini, one of the best special make-up effects artists in Paris, and we spent a lot of time making make-up effects for Super 8 movies in each other's garage or attic.

Growing up in the suburbs of Paris in the late 1980s and early 1990s, it was not as easy as it is today to get the right kind of information about the products and techniques needed for our trade. I ended up finding work experience in a small workshop in Paris under Michel Soubeyrand, where I learned a lot about mould-making, foam running, basic application techniques, and various useful tricks of the trade.

I worked on a couple of short films at that time, but my first break was offered to me by a friend's father, a theatre director who gave me the responsibility to design and build a whole range of animal masks for a musical he was putting together. After that I spent most of my 20s working for various theatre companies, building all sort of puppets, masks and various wacky contraptions.

I moved to Sydney, Australia, in 1998 and finally got a chance to work on the projects I was hoping to be a part of, like *The Matrix*, *Farscape* and *Star Wars*, among other things. I made my way back to Europe in 2005 to work in London on such projects as *Dr Who*, *Torchwood*, *Merlin*, *Harry Potter*, *Prometheus*, *World War Z*, *Maleficent*, *Thor: The Dark World*, *Guardians of the Galaxy*, and more to come…

I am now settled in London. If I am hired to develop characters and creature designs, I might work from home in my bedroom/office/sitting room as space is expensive here. If I am employed by a special make-up effects supervisor to work on a film, then I will spend my day in one of the London studios to design, sculpt or apply make-ups.

Although I work a lot, I also enjoy fishing, surfing, playing tennis, building things with Lego, and anything that allows me to spend time with my family. In the future, if I could find a way to work a bit less and have some more free time, and still be able to sustain my family, I would take it any time!

My advice to young artists wanting to break into the industry: Make sure you really, really, really want to do this, because you will have to spend a whole lot of time doing it before it starts paying off – and it might take a very long time!

feline predator

Q: What was your end goal when you first started this creature?

I saw a picture of a cheetah running … I love the dynamics and sleekness and speed of cheetahs. But I wanted to bring in a bit of roughness to the cheetah image, to bring in some hyena. I also wanted to resolve one of the main issues that cheetahs have – that they run out of breath. They can run really fast, but after a while they just can't breathe anymore. My creature has a hard top and a soft underbelly, and the underbelly opens up, not really like gills but almost, and facilitates gas exchange so the creature can breathe not only through its mouth but through its body. I thought that would be a cool way to keep the creature's engine running – so they can just keep on running.

Q: Did you start with the Creature Matrix to get your inspiration for this creature?

Yes, I took some elements from the matrix – the environment, the behavior – but then I went off it after a while.

Q: Apart from the matrix, what other inspirations did you have? You mentioned the cheetah and hyena, but was there anything else that really inspired you?

I stumbled upon this amazing image of a creature that looked a bit like a grasshopper, by a ZBrush artist named Grassetti. It was reminiscent of Yasushi Nirasawa's *Creature Core* art book. It had hardness and insect features but it bore a recognizable human-like shape. That was a key inspiration for me – the idea of taking a simple animalistic shape and cutting it, reorganizing it, and giving it another surface altogether. If you look at the silhouette from afar, it's not an unfamiliar shape. It's a principal that has worked for hundreds of years – four legs, a neck and tail, you get good balance, good motion, a set of teeth at the front, and off you go.

Q: Did you go through many variations or sketches or did you have a pretty clear vision of what you wanted in the end?

The drawn sketches were a study of the silhouette. I didn't want to explore the surface, the way it was broken down, I just wanted to study a general silhouette. It's not a hyena, it's not a cheetah or a leopard, it's something else which says 'mean' – with big teeth. I kind of went away from that in the end. What I find often when I design things is that I have to go through a lot of rubbish before I get to what I want to. It's a way to clarify where not to go. So, my original sketches look nothing like the end creature, but it's all part of the process.

Q: This character is clearly a predator. What does it hunt and what is its method of hunting?

It hunts in packs – that's why there are two in the image (only two from a larger pack). They are quite clever … they don't have a big brain but they work together pretty well. I wouldn't be surprised if these guys were living in the same universe as my third creature, the Harrysaurus, on a not-too-faraway planet, just a little way off our evolutionary path. Some of the characters in this book are just totally different – they are out there, but my creature is not like that.

Q: What did you try in terms of marking for hair, hide and teeth? Your character has a cool crest and almost mini tails. Can you describe some of those design and function elements?

The tail is a central core that pleats off in two pairs. I saw this as a way to enhance the creature's balance. The tails are probably furry at the end. The creature's back is a mixture of a hyena and the guy from *The Rocky Horror Picture Show*. There is something really creepy and awesome about hyenas – the way they are kind of manky. I didn't have a lot of time for exploration so I had to go for the first thing that worked for me, something solid. Simple colors. I think I had a couple of sketches with stronger markings … I also tried leopard spots at one point. If I had time, I might come back and touch up the final image a bit.

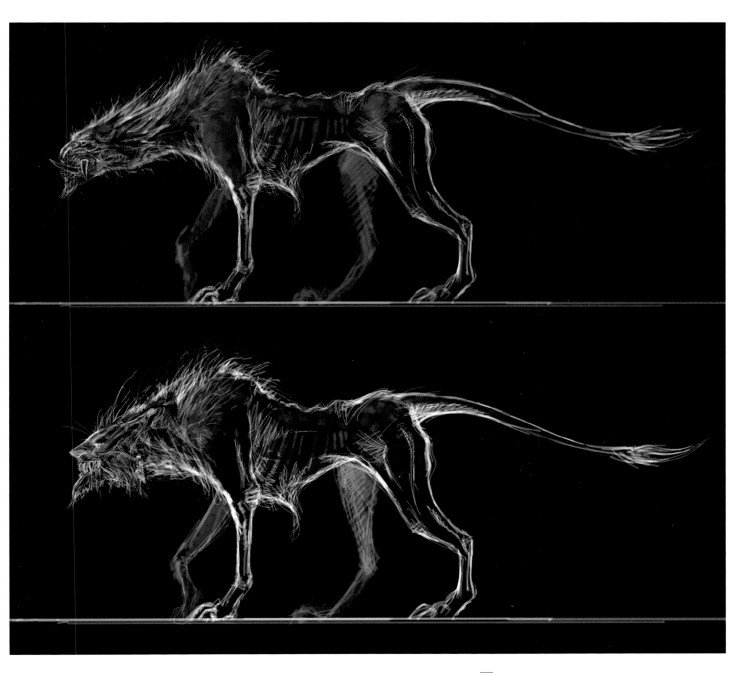

↑ Photoshop sketches focusing on the silhouette and the general lines.

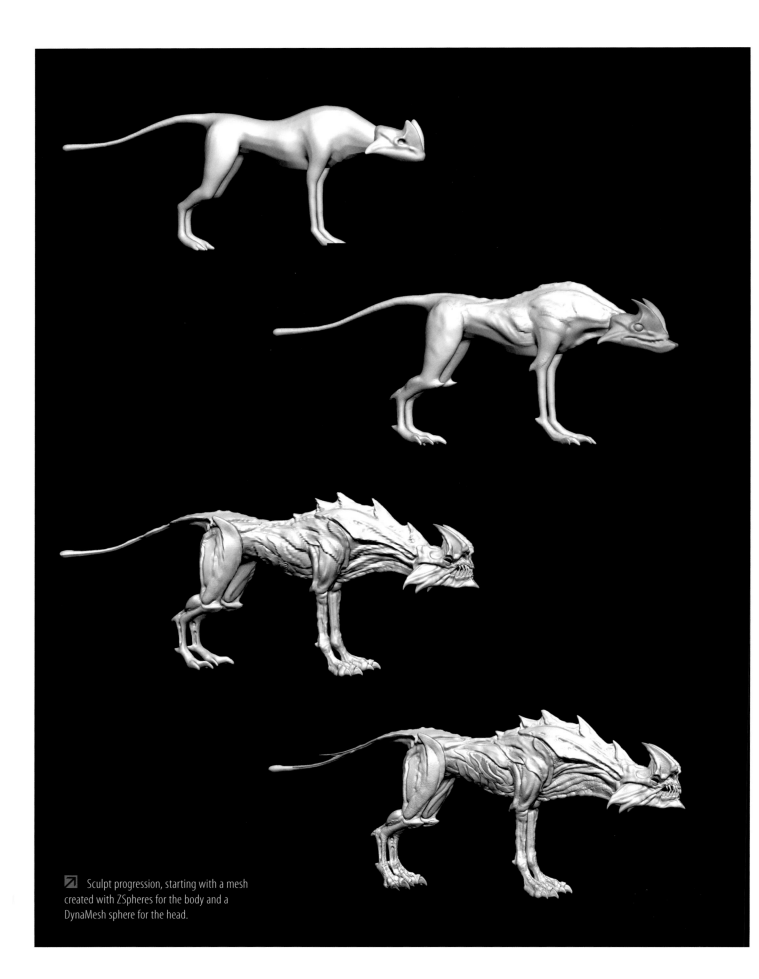

Sculpt progression, starting with a mesh created with ZSpheres for the body and a DynaMesh sphere for the head.

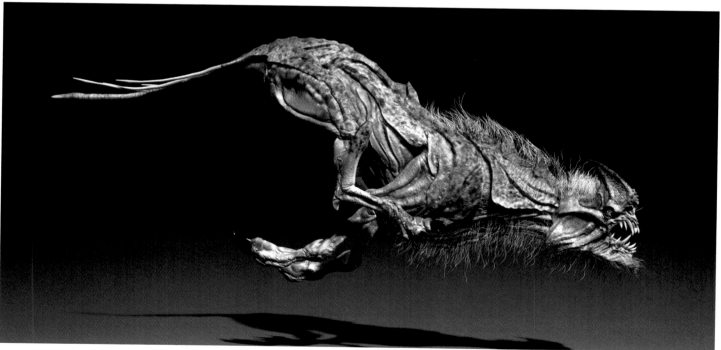

This page: First color test and render test after posing the model in a more dynamic attitude.

ambush snapper

MARTIN REZARD

Q: Tell us about this creature.

It's nothing like what I thought it would be when I started. My first idea was to have something that would be a predator of the polar bear, something that would hide in the icebergs, disguising itself as an iceberg, and feed on polar bear pups. But what I came up with was a bit reptilian, and I thought that a reptilian creature couldn't survive in such a cold environment … that wouldn't work at all.

Originally it was supposed to be quite large, like a small car, half rock but also ready to pounce … then it turned out more like a turtle. So I moved it out of the ice and into the jungle. The main drive was always for it to be camouflaged, and this camouflage became more grassy, rooty, which is why the creature's limbs became quite long and bent and out of shape. The limbs aren't really super-defined muscular limbs, but more like accidental rooty things hidden in the grass. Inside of that is the head, which actually doesn't really look like a head. This is a very patient creature, with a very slow metabolism; it can wait for its prey for as long as it needs … it waits for the right meal.

Q: Did the transition from an iceberg-hiding creature to jungle-hiding creature happen in your head or on paper?

It was more of a thought process rather than a series of sketches. I'm not a very fluent sketch artist … I'm used to ideas taking shape in the time that it takes for a sculpt to take shape. In the practical world, I'm a pretty fast sculptor – I can bring up shapes very quickly – but it's still a lot slower than sketching. I feed on the happy accidents that happen in the modeling process, which happen when you're working in water-based clay. This clay is very soft and flexible so you can bring things together very quickly and things happen that you hadn't planned. Then you can step back, look at it, and explore the interesting parts. I like to feed off that process. A lot of my friends have a very clear idea to start with and they sketch it quickly and then it's there, and then they move on to the next one, and the next one, etc. I'm a bit slower than that.

Q: This creature is clearly inspired by turtles and crustaceans … were there other inspirations?

There's a bit of frog in there as well, but it's quite crustacean in its shell, the protection on its back. Its underside is a bit softer, and it stays moist and keeps the muscles ready to pounce whenever they need to. I looked up snapping turtles and toads for inspiration. For the head I tried to break out a bit … the main shape for the head came from a fruit.

Q: Looking at your WIP images, the shape of the creature's shell changes quite a lot … at one point it's quite tall. What kind of process did you go through to determine the final shape of it?

It started quite tall because I wanted it to blend into an iceberg background … so I did something quite sharp and rock-like. Then it went closer to the ground and the vertical dimension was taken over by the plants growing on its back. This creature is the first one I started and the last one I finished, and it's been a struggle all the way.

Q: What were some of the things you struggled with, and how did you resolve them?

Trying to find a story behind it while trying to make it look interesting as a shape. I like the front limbs but I'm still not completely happy with the back limbs. The knees are a bit too basic. I would have done things differently with the back limbs if I had time. There are a lot of things I would have liked to address in different ways, maybe for the limbs to have multiple bones and very thin skin. I don't think I achieved exactly what I wanted on this creature, which is why I left it last to finish off. I would have liked to put more detail on it, but I was limited by time and the capacity of my machine. In the end this creature is more like an unfinished sketch that still has a lot to be resolved. It's not something I would sign off on.

Continued on page 210…

↙ ↘   This page: Sculpt in progress.
Body mesh created from ZSpheres and head
created from a DynaMesh sphere.

Q: Tell us about the head studies – what were you exploring there?

My original one was very turtle-like and I also wanted to bring something other worldly to it, something that wouldn't be so referential to something we all know. This is where the fruit reference came in. I stumbled upon a picture of a fruit in a book and I thought the aggressiveness of its shapes would easily translate into a predator's head shape. I was trying to get out of my comfort zone with the head, trying to come up with things I don't usually do. I was triggered by what I saw others in this book doing, and thought I could step out of my usual suit and do something else.

Q: Did you consider any variations – like male, female or a baby?

Not on this creature. I was entangled in sorting out the shape more than exploring variations. I didn't get halfway to where I wanted with this creature … it doesn't have all its DNA data present so I couldn't start coming up with variations. I was just trying to work out what was going on with it.

Q: What you ended up with looks like a really nasty, ground-based predator, one that you don't want to get within range of…

No, definitely not. Also, when you get close to him, he's not just ugly he's also very smelly, which is how he attracts his prey.

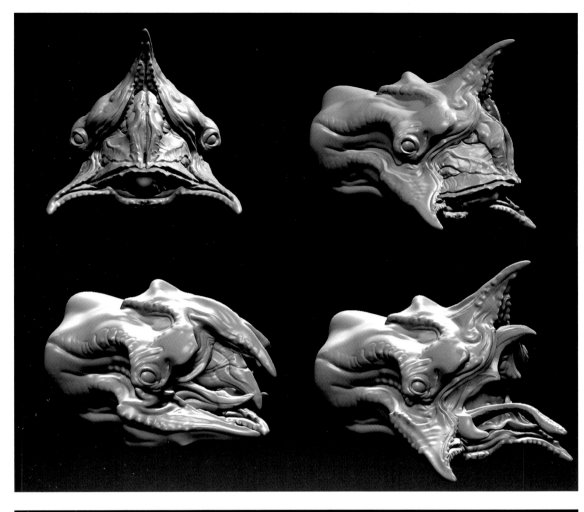

 Opposite page: Early attempt at placing the creature in a basic environment.

 Left: Study of possible head variations based on observation of a fruit. I wanted to move away from a turtle-like head and see what I could come up with.

Left: New head adjusted to the body.

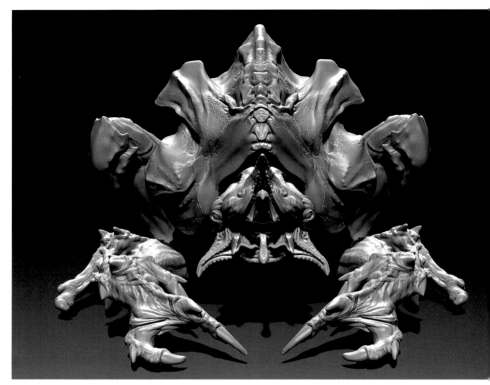

→ Right: Front view of the model in progress, with the mouth still wide open and the tongue sticking out.

↓ Below: Final creature with moss, grass and color. The arc of the back ended up coming down a lot from the earlier stages, mainly to make it easier for it to hide and blend into its surroundings.

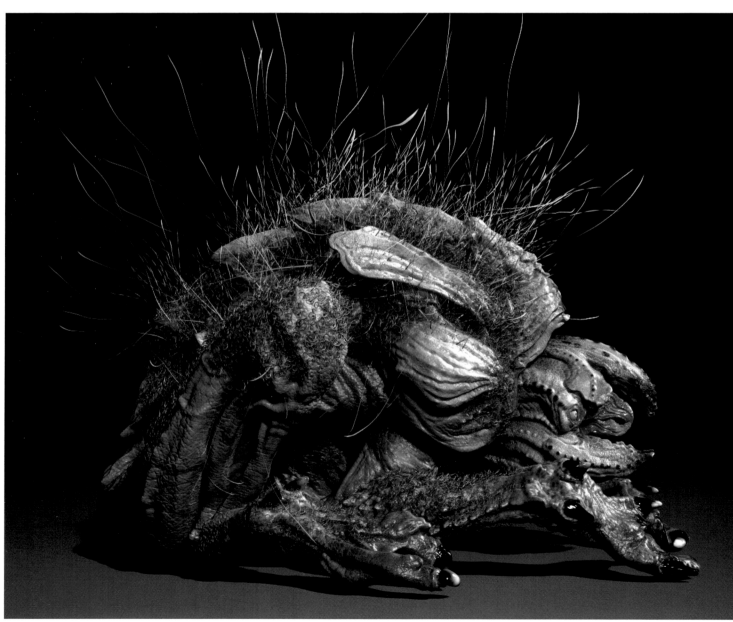

◄ Left: A view from underneath gives a bit more information about the anatomy of the beast.

▼ Below: Front view. I decided to have the mouth closed in the final image, to illustrate the creature waiting for its prey.

→ I presented the final render on a neutral background to make it easier to read as a shape.

harrysaurus

Q: Do you know someone called Harry?

Someone who left us recently and was a great inspiration to me.

Q: Of all of the different kinds of dinosaurs that we're familiar with, how did you decide to have something that roots around on the ground?

I've always had an absolute fascination for dinosaurs. I've always loved them and drawn them and sculpted them. I love their majesty and their wisdom – I love everything about them. I wanted to make one.

I was playing with different ideas to start with. I was thinking of pterosaurs, another predator maybe, but then I didn't want to have another predator because I already had a couple of predators on my list. I just wanted something gentle and nice and that would work in a herd, something that I could eventually create different types of – a youngster, an elderly one, a female one, which I ran out of time for. I have a 10-year-old son and we sit together and come up with great ideas; this idea was formed in partnership with him.

If you take out the spikes at the back, it's a lot like an anteater, with a long nose, long tongue, but it's also got elephant tusks and horns as well and that funny crested skull. It also has something that looks a lot like stegosaurus plates, but they're more open and wider at the back and have more layers. These are protective measures for it, they work in combination with its bright warning colors that say, "Don't eat me, I'm purple, I'm not going to be any good".

I wanted a nice plant-eating creature, quite elephant-like. I like the size of it. The black-and-white images on page 219 show good views from the back, front and the top – and there's something I really like about the top with all the layers, it's got a nice feel about it. This is why I provided the static images because they say a lot about the shape. As a sculptor I respond a lot to shape.

I've been in love with the stegosaurus since I was a kid – this creature is kind of the same idea but pushes it a bit further. With its funky head, this could be a missing link between dinosaurs and elephants.

Q: The back view is also a bit like a rhino – solid, built for power.

Yes. The back leans a lot longer than the front leans – it's all about balance, with the huge weight of the tail and all those plates that are sitting on the back end of the spine. When you've got such a huge amount of protection on your back, you need really, really strong back legs to carry them around and to move swiftly if you need to.

Q: Was there anything about the process you went through with this creature that was unusual, or was it a typical process for you?

It was a step-by-step exploration. In the first image it has a crest on the back of the head, which is very triceratops-like, which I got rid of very quickly and moved on to something else that would accommodate the horns working in conjunction with the tusks a bit more. I tried a couple of shapes … a lot of them went on the wayside but some of them are documented. I like the hard double crests, they are something I haven't seen a lot of … they are like brow bridges that are quite strong and horn-like and gather at the back of the head. I just love all of those things. To me they have the quality of fractal shapes, the way they display themselves and their color. I just absolutely adore those kind of shapes.

I was just trying to come up with something cool but which we haven't really seen before, but it's not completely out of this world either. It's still a cartoonish kind of creature but it's an exploration of what dinosaurs could have been I guess. This guy could live in the same world as the Feline Predator, but then the other two, the Ambush Snapper and the Jellybug, they live in another world.

Continued on page 218…

This page: Sculpt progression. The body mesh was created in ZSpheres then turned into a DynaMesh, and the head was started from a DynaMesh sphere.

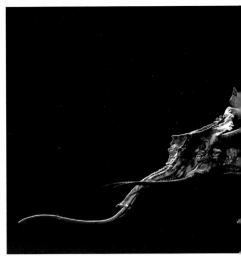

Q: With your color tests, the three are quite different. How did you analyze what was going on with the color and why did you end up with the colors you ended up with?

The reason I ended up with the final one is that it is softer, more gentle. The top one is quite black and red and has a hint of possible translucency in the plates, which I kind of like. This would probably apply to a large, dominant male, the colors saying, "Stay away, I'm not someone to mingle with". The purple one was a bit too colorful for me, and the middle one I was really trying to go gentle. So in the final image we might have a female and a youngster, and then the male would be a bit brighter, a bit redder, with probably stronger shapes and more defined horns on the head, an extra set of tusks or something like that. I wish I could have explored this more.

Q: It seems quite obvious for this creature to have a heavy, leathery hide, but did you contemplate any other textures, hair or anything?

No, I never imagined this guy with hair. It was pretty clear to me that it would have leathery, heavily folded skin. I couldn't see any reason to bring in hair. My son was trying to convince me to put on a really heavy ball on the end of the tail, but it didn't really work for me. I had to say no, and I hate to say no!

Q: In the final image, the background looks like an Australian bush scene…

I was looking for a waterhole or a place of gathering for my background image. One of my family members went on a trip to Central Australia recently and they took loads of pictures, so I sent them an email asking for some images of really beautiful landscapes. This landscape is from somewhere between Coober Pedy and Uluru.

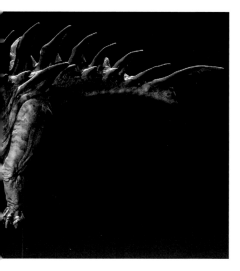

Above, left and opposite page bottom images: Final model before applying color. There is something really special about the view from above; the creature looks like a weird seahorse.

Top row: Color variations created in Photoshop on a grey render of the model exported from ZBrush. The red one on the left would probably be an alpha male.

jellybug

MARTIN REZARD

Q: Tell me about what you wanted to achieve with this character.

I had a very clear idea to start with. I was fascinated by the visual impact of the bluebottle, which is a sea predator – semi-translucent, very bright colors, a really beautiful creature but very nasty. I thought that if it works in the sea, why wouldn't it work in the air as well? What would happen if such lethal things were flying around in the air? What kind of hellish planet would that be? I started thinking about the idea of something that could inflate and deflate – with a hard-shelled front, sort of insectoid with small wings that can produce a gas lighter than the atmosphere so it hovers like a balloon with its long, highly poisonous tentacles floating around. The tentacles would be like fly-catchers, sticky paper that comes in a roll and catches small things on them. This creature would float around, with the help of its wings, and then go and harvest its dinner using its appendages. They could work in swarms and you could have hundreds of them around in the air – not a nice place for a walk.

I like the translucency, the bright colors of it, the luminescence. I tried to get all of it. I thought visually it would be an interesting creature. I think I captured my idea in the second image where it's flying … the luminescence isn't there but it's a bit more classical.

Q: Are you familiar with the book *The World of Kong* that came out from Weta after the movie?

Yes, they talk about how they developed an entire ecosystem. Even though many of those things didn't end up in the film, those that did end up in the film had incredible believability to them because they had been grown/developed in conjunction with other creatures in the ecosystem. It's a brilliant way to explore design.

Q: Did you explore things like camouflage and things like that?

Not really. I didn't do any color tests on this guy. There is a slight evolution between the first renders to the last ones. But the tonality was pretty much there at the start, with purple at the back to give it a kind of eeky-ness (a bit disgusting). There could have been a lot more happening with the color, but it ended up being what I could do in the time I had. The things I changed were lines and balance between the sack and the body and the wings. I was trying to stick to dynamic shapes, changing angles here and there, to give it a bit more attitude.

Q: The wings are quite like a dragonfly's wings. The creature doesn't have to support its weight, does it, the gas sack does that?

Yes, the gas sack gives it buoyancy and then it relies on draughts. The wings are more there for direction, I suppose. They started off quite big, too big, then I shrunk them right down to give more importance to the sack, which is what actually gives it its ability to fly around. It's more like an inflatable balloon, really. It can gather a bit of speed with its wings, but it's not a chaser, it's not aggressive, it just flies around and catches whatever is silly enough to be in that place at the time.

Q: Was there any particular part in this process where you got stuck? How did you get over it?

No, this one was really straightforward. I took it to a certain stage and then moved on to something else so I could think about it for a while. By the time I got back to it, it had evolved. The proportions changed quite a lot between versions, and the inflatable sack ended up taking on more importance in the later versions. The end product is quite close to my original idea.

Very often when I'm hired to design things and I've been given a brief for something, the first idea needs to be pulled out and put away, and the second idea is the thing you really want to go for, and then you do a few more to give people some choices. But I think one of the first ideas is often the one you should go for – that works best for me. I don't believe in going over and over a design. Usually the

222 creative essence: creatures

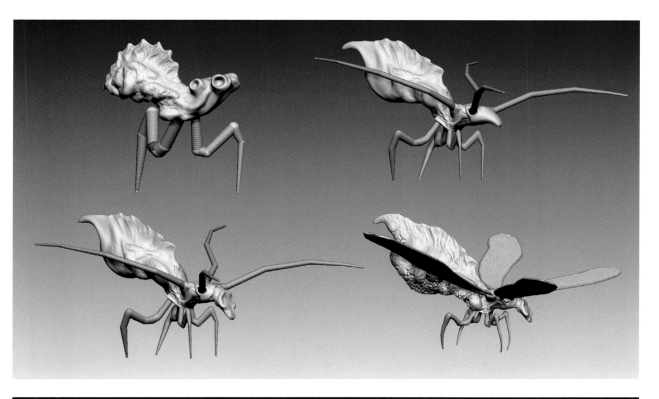

This page: Progression of the sculpt, done in ZSpheres and DynaMesh. The tentacles where generated using FiberMesh.

first or second drafts are full of enthusiasm and passion and, after a while, if you go over and over the same thing, you lose that. I like it when my first ideas are picked up – that makes me happy.

Q: I notice with your WIP *[bottom image this page]* **the eyes are quite distinctly different to the ones in your earlier WIPs … How did that happen?**

They just popped out. I saw some amazing pictures of a turtle ant … my first head was quite close to that of a turtle ant. Then I wanted to give my creature the look of it moving, darting around, constantly on the hunt. I thought having the eyes on stalks would be a good addition to it, and kind of balance out the huge weight of the sack at the back.

Q: **You also went away from fairly straight hanging tentacles to ones that look almost frizzy…**

All the pictures I was referencing regarding the bluebottle show these animals always sitting on a current or moving, they are very rarely just hanging down. So I changed the tentacles to give a sense of motion to the whole image.

Q: **In the final image the tentacles have little hairs on them. How did they get developed?**

The first ones were single strands of tentacles. After I extracted them from ZBrush and started playing with them in Photoshop, I instinctively started making them a bit sharper, like thorns, to give them a better chance of catching things. They are actually fibermesh hair generated in ZBrush. You can generate second-generation fibermesh on the original fibermesh, and create hair within hair within hair. I thought it would look sharper and harder – these are all the poisonous little bits, so this enhances the chances of anything getting caught in there. This creature is like a flying poisonous net.

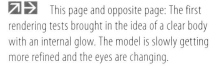 This page and opposite page: The first rendering tests brought in the idea of a clear body with an internal glow. The model is slowly getting more refined and the eyes are changing.

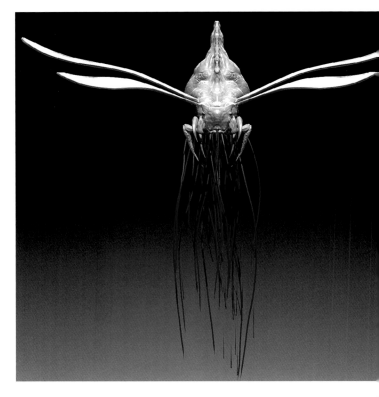

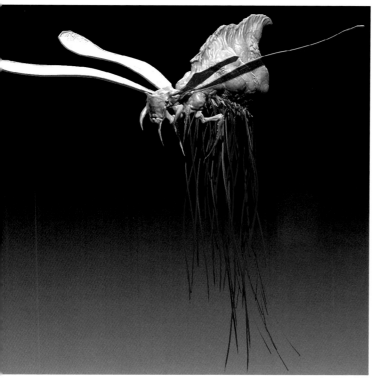

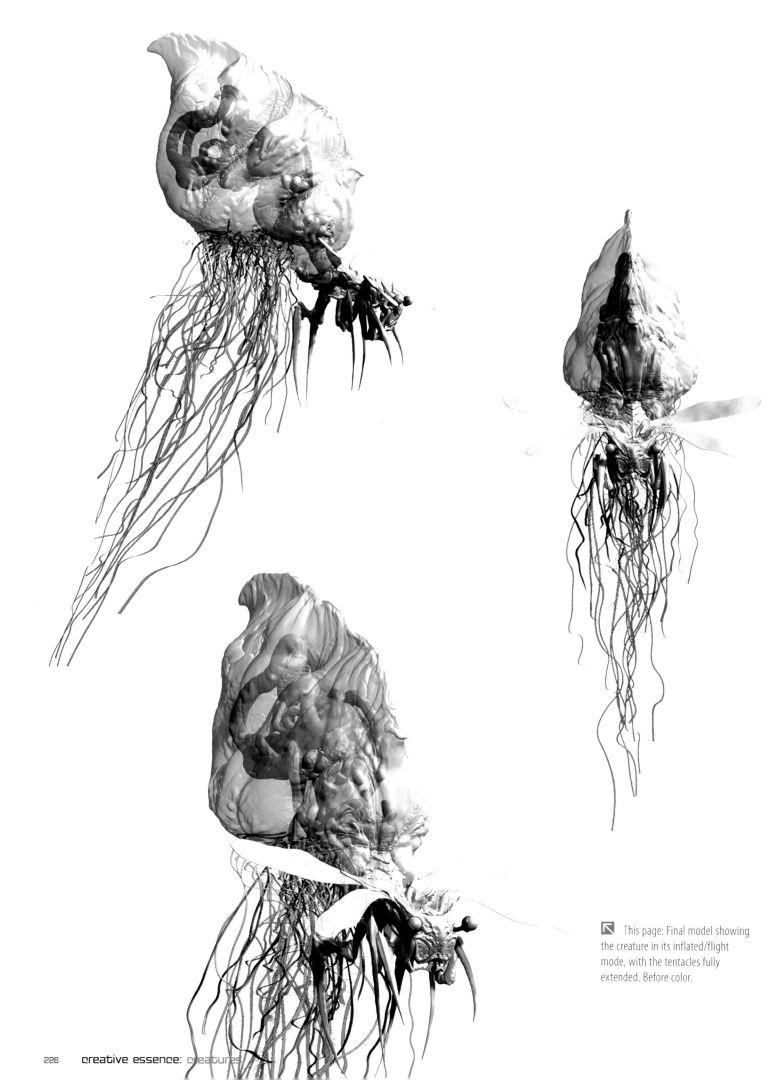

This page: Final model showing the creature in its inflated/flight mode, with the tentacles fully extended. Before color.

This page: Final model showing the creature in its deflated/landing mode, with the tentacles retracted within the sack.

↑ Above: The Jellybug is resting and is deflated.

→ Right: The Jellybug is inflated and on the move.

simon webber

For as long as I can remember, I was always day-dreaming, wondering about and questioning the nature of things and people. I think the first notion I had of knowing I wanted to create things was being mesmerized by late 1970s sci-fi movies such as *Star Wars* and *The Black Hole*. In particular, the robots in *The Black Hole* fascinated me and I think led to my later interest in animatronics.

My first professional insight into the world of creature and character design came from doing school work experience at Jim Henson's Creature Shop when I was 14. I had written a letter to Jim himself, and, shortly after, received a reply inviting me to spend a few weeks at the company's main workshop, which at the time was based in a large ex-postal sorting office in Hampstead Heath, North London. Those two weeks were absolutely amazing to me and amounted to one of the most inspiring times in my life, creatively. I spent my lunch hours studying old sculptures that were lying around, leftover from productions like *The Dark Crystal, Labyrinth* and *The StoryTeller*. It certainly beat working a cash register at the local supermarket. Sadly, a short time before my work experience started, Jim died suddenly of pneumonia.

In the 12 years following art school I pursued a career in special make-up effects before transitioning to character design work. The second movie I ever worked on – *Saving Private Ryan* – was another experience I will never forget. Once, I stayed up after doing a night shift on location in Wexford, Ireland, to watch the day's shooting, which happened to be a major

sequence of the film's opening scene depicting the Normandy landings of World War II. There were mortars rocketing sand and water 15 feet above our heads as Tom Hanks and his troops were crawling in the sand just a few yards in front of us, while Spielberg and his crew gave direction and planned the shot. Later, we watched as stuntmen in full GI attire fled a flaming landing boat, all this amid thick smoke and explosions. It was AMAZING! I remember a friend saying he felt sorry for me in a way because I was starting out on the biggest movie I would probably ever work on and that it would be 'all downhill' after that … but then we followed that up by working on *Gladiator*! You never know what is around the corner.

Aside from some close colleagues, I don't really have any mentors as such but there are many people who have and continue to inspire me. They are figureheads in their respective fields and include all the usual suspects within the practical effects industry such as Rick Baker for the overall high quality of his work and art direction, Rob Bottin for his unbridled imagination, the late Stan Winston for his ability to create iconic characters, and Steve Johnson for his constant innovation. I also look up to many other artists, from illustrators to film directors, the likes of Mœbius, Zdzisław Beksinski, HR Giger, Dali, Stephen Spielberg, Hayao Miyazaki, Jim Cameron, Ridley Scott, and the classical artists Michaelangelo, Rodin and Da Vinci.

Aside from my work, I used to play bass in various bands, but these days I'm usually too tied up with work to fit in any real practise. Movies are a big part of my spare time, though. These days I find myself moving away from the diet of big summer blockbusters and the low-budget monster-schlock I grew up on, and tend to watch more independent films.

I would say to young artists who want to break into this industry: Be sure it's really what you want to do because it can sometimes be a rocky road. I think in a lot of the commercially creative industries it is often a case of 'feast or famine' – good times (steady, regular work that you enjoy) can often be followed by months of hard times (no work at all) and vice versa. So it can be tough at times but if you're in it for the right reasons and are self-driven, this won't matter so much. Also, if you can, save money for the slow times. The CG industry today is an increasingly competitive industry and it seems that speed is a highly regarded attribute to possess … but speed should never take the place of quality. A steady quality of work is more likely to guarantee success in the long run, and, even if it doesn't, you'll have the peace of mind that comes from knowing your work was solid.

the healer

Q: Where did you start your thinking process for this creature?

I had a recurring idea that I thought would be interesting, which relates to both of my creatures – one man's food is another man's poison … the universe wastes nothing, that kind of idea. You've got this creature that feeds off bad enzymes or poisons or toxins, dead tissue and skin cells from another creature … The Healer takes all the bad stuff out of dying or damaged organisms and converts it into something else for its own good.

Sometimes in my work I have very specific briefs, other times I am given little to no brief, people just want to see what you come up with. In those cases, I'll usually push around a bit of digital clay and something will come together quite quickly. I did that for a few of these creatures, letting the forms come together in front of me, which would start to dictate a direction. Then I would look for some shapes – this is looking a bit crab-like or that looks desert-dwelling – and that would then feed back to me and then I'd feed that back into the sculpt.

Q: Did you find that the Creature Matrix was helpful at all?

I found it good to know it was there, but I had so many ideas of my own I wanted to explore and I went off in all different directions. I had a look at the matrix, and some of the routes on there were places I wanted to explore anyway. It's an interesting way to start to look at creature design.

Q: With this creature, you were saying you were just pushing some digital clay around…

Yes, but I had this idea of what I wanted him to be in the beginning … this sort of janitor dude who goes around fixing broken life forms.

Q: Did you start with a face or a body type?

I was blocking in his head and his upper torso, and that

came together pretty quickly, then I tried out different arms and things. I used to do special make-up effects, which involved quite a bit of traditional sculpting in clay … I'm from more of a sculpting background than drawing. So programs like ZBrush enable me to produce illustrations, because my strength is 3D forms. I blocked in his head and upper torso and had an idea that I wanted him to be bulb-headed in a classic pulp alien-type way, and from a damp environment – an amphibious dude.

When I did make-up effects, my focus was always on trying to make things organic and softening things off. But then on a job a couple of years ago I was working with a great group of artists, drawing all these dynamics lines, and they were doing the opposite of what I used to do – everything was more angular. So these days I try to start with bolder forms because I know they'll soften out along the way.

This creature started off a bit more rigid, once I started blocking his arms in. I wanted to do something with alternative anatomy, with double sets of arms, and to have the middle set of arms cloaked with fatty, toad-like skin. I started adding the separate elements to him once I had the head and the torso in place. Usually once I get to texturing then that stuff sort of falls into place for me – that's something I used to do a lot in make-up effects, so it's usually just a case of following the contours of the forms. I was trying to get some dynamic shapes in there at the beginning but wanted to keep a Martian- and frog-like essence in there, too.

Q: When you design a creature like this, do you think about how it might move, sound and eat, and does that inform your design process?

Definitely. I have seen a lot of work that has style over content. I come from a background where you have to actually make the things you design, so there is an almost blueprint element to it. I always try to think about what's going on underneath the skin and fat layers, etc., because form follows function. You can take a bit of creative license with the biology of course, but if an animator had to animate it, there would be enough for them to work with

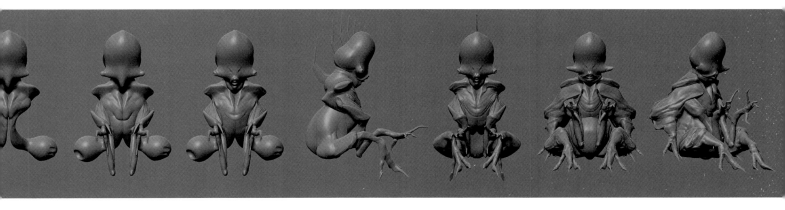

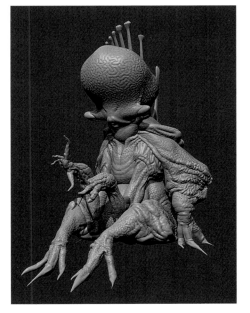

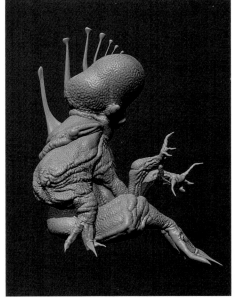

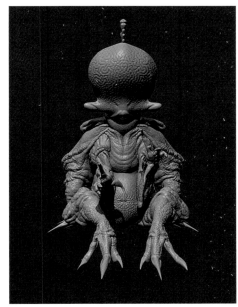

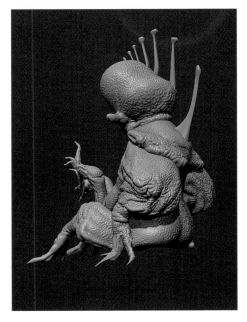

 Top row: Initial ZBrush sculpt development.

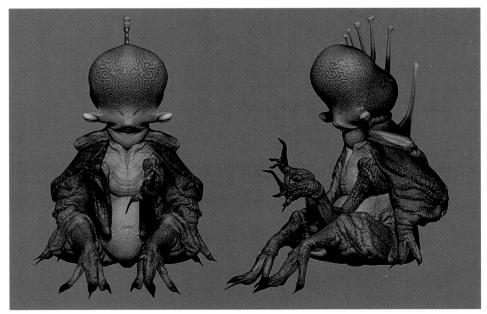

Rest of page: Development of the textures in ZBrush, cloaking the middle set of arms with fatty, toad-like skin. First Polypaint color pass.

that wouldn't break the laws of physics and biology.

I dip into all sorts of references in my head – nature books that I've seen and other artist's work – but I try not to have those references out in front of me otherwise I can end up inadvertently copying them. I just act on a feeling and go from there. Only if I'm really stuck on how the texture or something should go will I get out a book.

Q: When you start thinking about textures, did you have an idea of what end point you'll get to, or did this one just grow and evolve?

He definitely evolved. I didn't have an idea of exactly how he'd look at the end. He evolved to a point where it's more than I had planned in terms of textures and things … I took it further than what I was thinking originally. Initially I don't think I was going to take the bioluminescent back spines so far … at one point they were just going to be regular spines, not glowing. I also really worked on the fatty, toad-like skin hanging on his outer arms. I wanted a leather-like, drapery feel around some of its limbs, almost implying clothing, Japanese/samurai clothing, with tight bands around the wrists and elbows with big billowing bits of flesh. I took that further than I had initially planned, too, and I'm quite happy with how it has turned out.

Q: He looks like a really sedentary creature but he's got these big nasty looking claws…

I don't think I put too much thought into the tips of his toes and fingers, they just ended up the way they are. I'm glad that they're like that … but it is in contrast to the friendly toad/frog element. The hands on his middle arms, the ones he's reaching out to the flower with, I saw them as dexterous rather than nasty. They are kind of creepy and odd-looking but they're not nasty – they are tinkerer's hands with an alternate anatomy. I like that the tips of his toes and fingers have a bit of an edge. Essentially he's one of the good guys, it's just unfortunate for him that his appendages look a bit creepy…

Q: Tell us a bit about the process you used for this creature. Was it a normal work process for you or did you try something different?

Some people have their pipelines but I don't really – I like to

try different things, to keep things fresh. I'll often just push a shape around for a bit and if it's not working I'll start another one. There's a fairly recent addition to ZBrush called DynaMesh where you can smash meshes together and unify them really quickly. I really like it and use it a lot. Using DynaMesh is essentially how it would work in the real world – smashing bits and pieces together and building things up gradually. So sometimes I'll work like that and other times I'll block in the whole thing with ZSpheres – block out the whole shape all in one. I like having them in pieces so I can switch them out. If, for example, I realize halfway through that the arms are wrong, I can lose them – I don't have to chop a bit off the mesh, I can just turn off that particular subtool.

With this creature, I focused on the face and the torso first. Sometimes you need to work on the face to find the character and then it spreads out from there. I got his core and his head pretty much in place, then I roughed in some arm shapes. With this guy I actually didn't use DynaMesh much, instead I kept all the pieces separate.

Q: Tell us about your ideas for his environment. At one point you described him as a bit of a guru sitting up on a high place. Where did that idea come from?

I saw him as almost like the cobbler's elves that come in to fix things … he's around but you'd have to look really hard to see him. He has a strange presence … he's reclusive, he just comes in and does his thing when no one's around and no one's really aware of him.

Q: What was the idea with the rocks, rather than him being in a cave or in a forest?

I guess there is an element of a Tibetan monk up in the mountains type thing going on. That was just a feeling really. Usually creature designs are placed in one of several very stereotypical environments … I wanted to try something different. I also wanted to have some sky in there, but I ended up ditching that and he doesn't look as high up or solitary as I had planned in my head. I was going to emphasize how high up he was by having some sort of pterodactyl-type bird in the background but decided not to make it more difficult for for myself because I had a lot of other creatures planned.

Q: **Looking at your final image, the spines on his back have glowing ends like in the earlier images, but right at the last step you've introduced what look like glowing spores coating his shoulders. Was that an idea you had at the beginning or did it come in late?**

I think it came in late. Looking at the image, I was happy with the wrinkly texture that was draping around his shoulders, but I felt like the spines with the glowing tips were coming out of nowhere and didn't tie in with anything else. I felt like something was needed somewhere else, and I didn't want to put anything on the opposite end of his body, which would make them seem tagged on. The shoulders felt like the right place.

Q: **Can you tell us about the flower?**

I think the flower was actually a time-saver. I wanted him to be either releasing a creature he's healed or a flower that he's rejuvenated – and the flower was the easiest and quickest option. In a way, the flower is more peaceful and trippy … I like how it works. I'm not sure how clear it is that he's healing the plant or whether it seems like it's a magical flower … either way, I like the general vibe of the image.

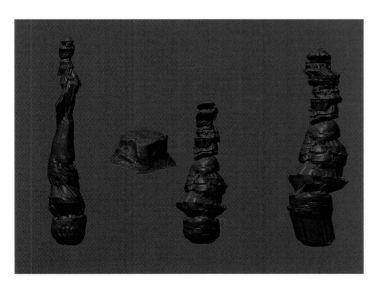

Above: Low poly block outs for the stalagmite rock formations of the environment.

Above images: Composition tests with rocks, and further color development.

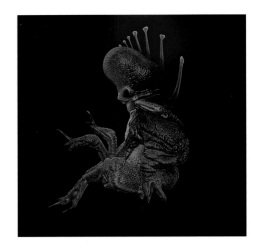

→ Right: A quick
bioluminescence color test.

↑ Above: A light and background test, which
also helped me decide against the addition of
glowing eyes.

→ Right: A mood-light test.

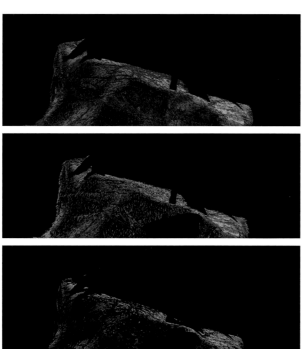

Above: Addition of vegetation, using ZBrush's
FiberMesh, lightening of the face, and blending all
of the elements together.

Left images: Rock moss options, rendered as
separate elements.

The final result.

agonia pulchra

Q: **What were your initial thoughts about this creature? Did you have an end goal in mind?**

I was a bit hazy on its direction at first, then I thought that if this thing could fly it would be more of a threat … you can't just jump on it to kill it. So I thought I'd introduce some wings. Once I started playing around with some colors, it started developing more of an *Avatar* vibe. I thought I could make it not just menacing but hypnotic, in terms of all the crazy color patterns going on. I spent way too long messing around with the color variations because it was fun, and I started to lose sight of what I wanted to do with it. Once I started seeing it as a really nasty butterfly, I got the idea of it being something from deepest, darkest Africa or the equivalent in another world. After that I started thinking of it as being an artifact of unknown origin, in a museum. I had this idea of things in jars, museum artifacts, with no one knowing anything about them. Then I started moving more in that direction.

Q: **What inspired your ideas for this creature?**

I was just pulling around some shapes to begin with. I knew I wanted something very nasty or venomous, that could kill you, but nothing more than that really. I wanted something that looked like you really don't want to touch it – it's 'stabby', your average nasty beetle archetype, the size of a small lobster. Once I started playing with the colors and patterns, the thought process started to develop and move in a specific direction.

Q: **It looks like you settled on a form fairly quickly, then your experimentation really seemed to happen in terms of the coloring…**

Exactly. It's quite interesting how even though it's only colors and patterns, that you can take something from being drab and understated to something more vivid and outlandish – a 'make-over' in one step. I do think this creature became less hardy with the addition of the wings, though. I like the simplicity of it without wings, as you can see the form better. So, the final image isn't the best from

a form standpoint, but I think psychologically it has more going for it … there's more to fear.

Q: **With the color variations, what's your normal process with that? Where do you start? Does the color you start with come from the creature or do you think from the start, "I want something red or green"?**

I used masking on the sculpt as a guide for the paint job, embellishing the forms that were there, and I also referenced some blue crabs amongst other things. Once I had this fleshy looking crab guy with blues, yellows and whites as a color base, I generated some color maps and started playing around with variations, which gradually got crazier and crazier. I used different layer styles with the maps in Photoshop – I'd merge two layer styles to generate a new one, and overlay that on to another layer with yet another layer style. I did lots of experimenting. Then I'd throw them back on to the model to see which ones worked and which ones didn't. Usually I could tell which colors or patterns were going to work beforehand.

Q: **How did you choose the end one?**

I think I ran out of steam actually! I had so much fun trying out different options, and there were several versions that I liked equally. I think I settled on the final one because it was fairly easy on the eye and I liked the idea that this thing is lethal but really attractive. I don't think the final one is necessarily the best one but it seemed more 'real world'. For its label, I started to think about how often some of the more arcane artifacts found in museums are written in Latin, so I was looking at Latin words to name it. At one point I was thinking about using the word *ignotus*, which means 'unknown' in Latin.

Q: **The fact that it can fly adds to its scariness – so it's not just going to crawl up your leg, it could come from anywhere…**

I saw it as something between a crustacean and an insect

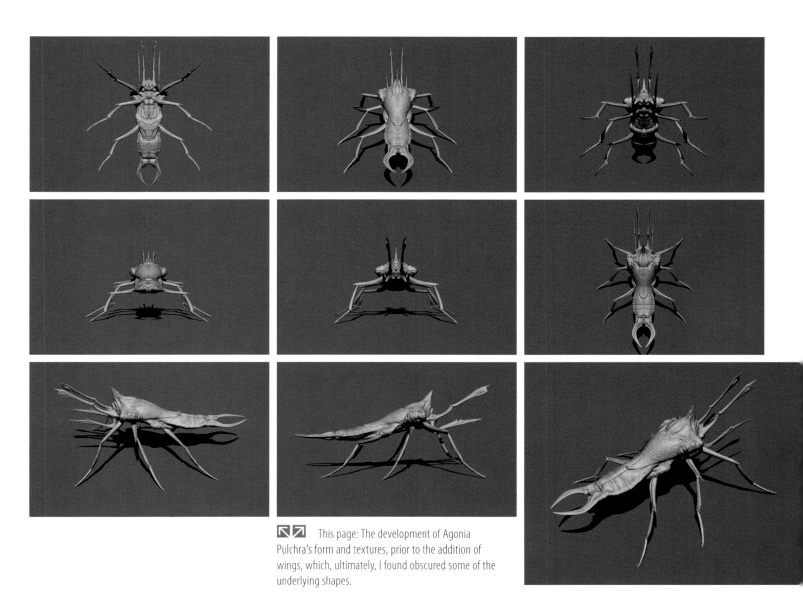

⬉⬈ This page: The development of Agonia
Pulchra's form and textures, prior to the addition of
wings, which, ultimately, I found obscured some of the
underlying shapes.

so, although it's got wings, it shouldn't be seen as delicate – it's armored. A few summers ago I was walking down the street one evening and I heard what sounded like a Chinook helicopter flying right past my ear … it was a stag beetle. I'd never seen them fly before, but the theme I got from it was that this thing was armor-plated and was airborne, and almost seemed to defy physics because it was so stocky. So, although this creature has wings and looks pretty, it's solid. It's not a case of just chasing it across the floor … it can go anywhere really. Be afraid…

Q: When you're in the middle of a design process and you get stuck, what methods do you have to get you past these points?

These days if I hit one of those walls, I'll sometimes switch to working on another character to take my mind away from it. Either that or I go in a completely different direction, which often yields results as well. I'm not really a quitter so usually I keep trying to fight through those moments when it's not working.

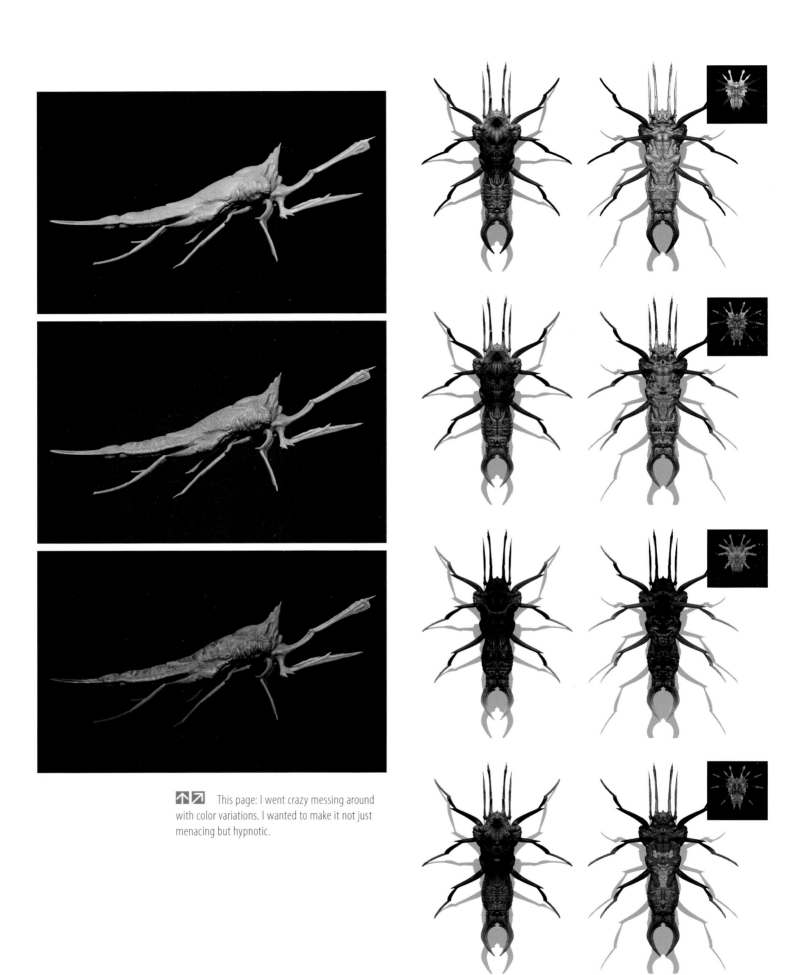

↑ ↗ This page: I went crazy messing around with color variations. I wanted to make it not just menacing but hypnotic.

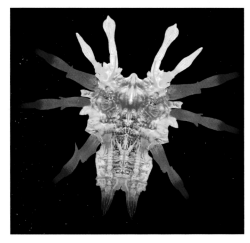
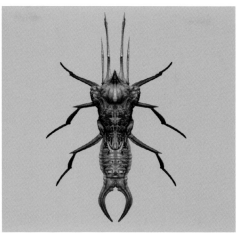

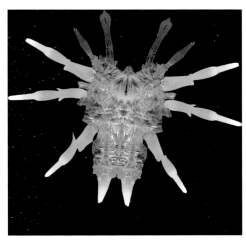

This page: More color experimentation.

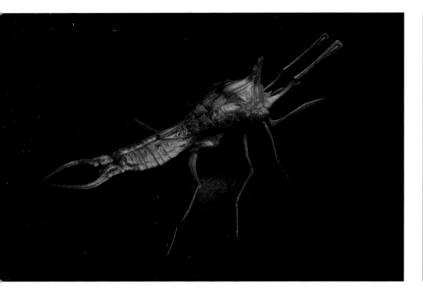

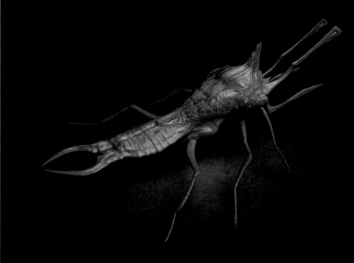

↑ Above row: These four examples show how the impact of a creature can be changed just using color.

↑ Above: I introduced some wings and started seeing it as a really nasty butterfly or lobster — or a 'lobsterfly'.

→ Opposite page: From one of my other concepts, I had this idea of things in jars, of unknown origins, in a museum.

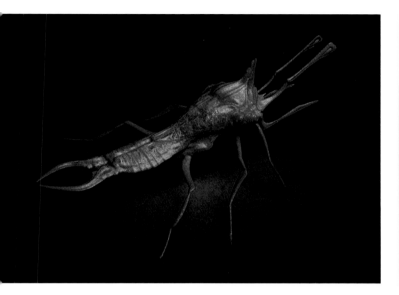

➜ The final image of Agonia Pulchra in a museum display case.

other concepts

⬆ Jar X

⬆ Bulbfish

These sketches, speed sculpts and designs are ideas that didn't make it past the early ideation stage, but present exciting would-be creatures and concepts to explore in the future.

⬆ Squatter   ⬇ Cave Lurker

⬆ Spearhog

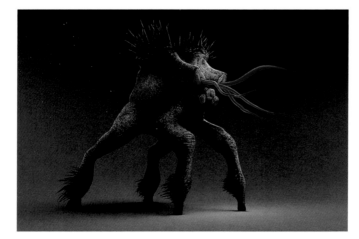

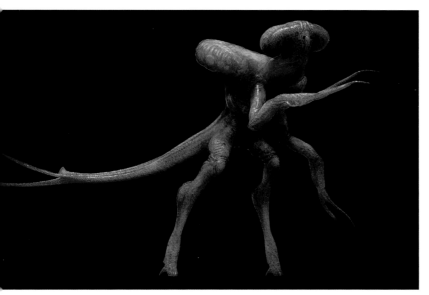

Blood Tickler

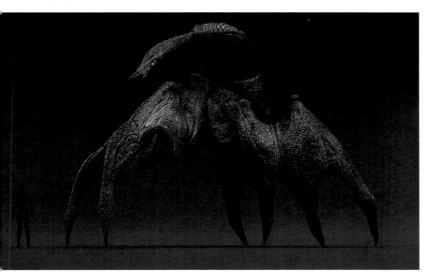

Curveback

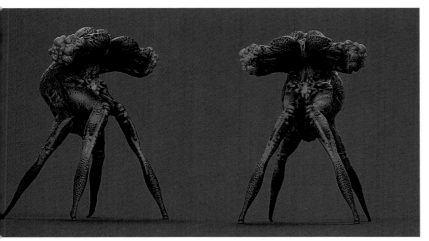

Spongia Vorax

Octoboxer

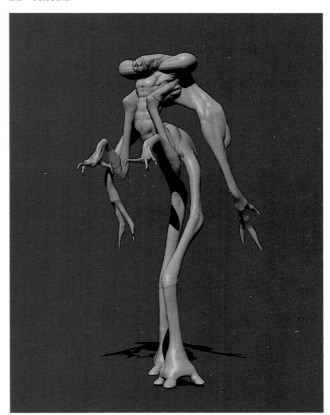

Strider

Creative Essence: The Face – Lighting and Rendering Monica

The Weeping Woman, Carlos Ortega Elizalde, MEXICO

Creative Essence

THE FACE

EXPOSÉ 11

VIEW OUR OTHER TITLES ON OUR WEBSITE

Ballistic Publishing publishes the finest digital art in the known universe.

Be inspired by thousands of images from the world's leading digital artists! Ballistic Publishing is an award-winning publisher. Our books will inspire and educate you. For 'best of' digital art, our *EXPOSÉ* books are unsurpassed. Our *d'artiste* range features the techniques of master artists and includes biographies, extensive galleries of their work, and a range of tutorials in which each artist explains their overall approach and strategies that work for them. With our *Art of the Game* series, *Exotique* and the *Creative Essence* series, Ballistic Publishing is sure to have something for everyone.

Visit: **www.BallisticPublishing.com**

/ BALLISTIC /

WWW.BALLISTICPUBLISHING.COM